Hi mums, dads, carers, grandparents, teachers and friends, this book is for you if

- You want a kid to thrive in our wo

- You would like to resolve worries,

- You wish your child would co-operate more and be easier to live with.

- You want to swap negative actions or behaviours for effective communication - especially of scared, angry or sad feelings.

- You have a happy child and you would like this to continue as they grow up.

- You want to confidently support them in the most nurturing and loving way.

- You would like to understand a kid's distress and know how best to help.

- You like your child feeling self-assured, managing home and school well, and still having time to just be themselves, for laughter and fun.

Mums, dads, carers and others: This handbook is for making family life less stressful, easier and more enjoyable, and childhood happier for loads of kids. It is written for parents of kids aged about 4–11, but can be adapted to any age.

Teachers: Even understanding 'Owl and Cat' types will make life easier for you in your classroom.

Grandparents: Enjoy these ideas and approaches with your grandchildren, and your adult son or daughter. Leave mums and dads to be with their kids in their own way.

I wish you all the very best, Felicity

What people are saying about this book

'I found the Understanding part beautiful. It was a pleasure to read and extremely useful.'
Claire, mum of three.

'Reading this book puts me back on track.'
Alison, childminder, mum of teenagers, one with Asperger's.

'Emily is continuing to do really well. In fact, she is thriving. I continue to be blown away by the ongoing changes in her. She is an absolute delight to have around and a very different girl from how she was - even before she became unwell. You were absolutely right that she is a very intelligent girl. We have some wonderful discussions about all sorts of things: religion, animal welfare, human rights and social equality issues. She is fun, kind and caring and has a great sense of humour. She has a number of very good friends. At gatherings, she is literally the life and soul of the party, amazing our adult friends as she goes up to them for a chat and a hug! The whole family is benefiting from Felicity's 6 Step approach.'
Jane and Rob, solicitor, parents of three.

'When I first met Felicity in 2012, she simply 'saw' my children for who they were! It was life changing and completely liberating. Felicity encouraged me to be the parent I wanted to be: honest, fun, exciting, trustworthy and loving. The Handbook for 21st Century Mums and Dads perfectly encompasses Felicity's philosophy of being present, honest and loving with your kids. It is an invaluable tool in today's busy, modern world and is sure to create new, meaningful connections in all families.'
Natasha, mum of four. Find Natasha's blog at unschoolingaspies.blogspot.com - an Avenue Mum blogging the differences.

'The Handbook for 21st Century Mums and Dads is an invaluable resource in helping children and families to be at peace with themselves and to develop lasting qualities of kindness and caring. Felicity generously shares her wisdom and experience along with many tried and tested strategies - an invaluable purchase for busy parents!'
Geoff Smith, headteacher and author of The Primary Character Curriculum.

'Super interesting to read about the Cat/Owl Children. I really see that Hendrix has strong Cat traits and how being aware of this not only helps him to progress through each day, but the way I communicate with him.'
Jamie, dad of two, Azulfit for health and wellbeing www.azulfit.com.

'For years, in workshops and private sessions, I've referred parents and therapists dealing with challenging children to Felicity Evans and her amazing, groundbreaking centre, NatureKids. Felicity understands the needs of today's children better than anyone else I've come across. She knows that the parenting model we inherited from our parents can do more harm than good with these children and her life's work has been to teach parents how to parent in a new way. This book should be in every antenatal clinic so that new parents can start using these methods right from the beginning.'
Ann Callaghan, homeopath and producer of Indigo Essences for Children.

Felicity Evans

Felicity is a teacher and family support counsellor who has worked with children at a grass roots level for many years, helping babies to thrive, toddlers to talk, kids to communicate and learn, and young people and university students to succeed.

She has acquired many ways to support children during her career: a nursery school assistant at 16; a teacher where her passion for communication and building a sense of self started; a Deputy Head in a hospital school; a SENCO; writing her own programme for dyslexic children -The Other Path.

From 2000 she welcomed many children to her centre, NatureKids. Some parents wanted to offer their children different experiences in education. Other children came to overcome distress in school or at home. Many had communication differences or found it difficult to learn and some had addictions.

Labels like ADHD, autism, anxiety and depression may give useful information about our children but they are not always bringing them the understanding, support and compassion they need.

Felicity especially wants to take away the stigma of these labels, as her approaches have not only brought many children and young people to happiness and achievement, but also enriched her life.

This handbook has come from these years of experience and the insights she gained at NatureKids. This diverse mixture of children became a 'family', welcoming new arrivals and staying friends after they left. They want to change previous patterns that no longer work, to manage their basic skills and to reveal their unique talents. These kids want to empower the world with their love and passion.

Moment by moment, Felicity learnt about the inner journey these kids have to accomplish, often to come out of huge heartache into a norm of happiness..

It is an absolute joy for Felicity to share what she has learnt from all the children and to pass it on to you through this book

Supporting differences, overcoming challenges

This book comes from being with my son, Iestyn, all the NatureKids and every child I have ever met.

It is written with profound thanks to all the kids for teaching me so much and bringing me wisdom and joy.

I offer what I have discovered to the mums and dads and carers of today. Thank you for having such amazing children to enrich all our tomorrows.

I would like this book to reach every child so that their happiness far outweighs their heartache.

———————

Many thanks to all of you who have helped me with this book:

Chris Day, Jane Mallin and everyone at Filament and Clare Clarke at www.fusion3media.co.uk

Millie Townsend, I really appreciate your creating wonderful pictures which illustrate my points so well.

Claire McKenzie, I am so grateful for your time, your incredible aptitude at helping me to express myself clearly and your understanding and support for this book.

Dr. Claire McKenzie, collaborative and substantive editing. Email: flux13@hotmail.com

Alison Downs, you did a grand job gently leading me from knowing only the very basics about computers to managing OK on my own – some of the time!

Thanks to Jackie Burwell, Lesley Barry and everyone who enabled NatureKids to thrive over the years – staff, families and friends. We are grateful to our team of professionals who helped us with the kids – there are links to them in the Resources of this book.

Thank you to my neighbours including Joe Hayes, who kept the farmhouse ticking over and gave a sense of calm, Karyn Hill in the States and all the friends who openly chatted to me about children. I often smiled and said – 'That's in my book'.

Cover photo and portrait: Hannah Couzens www.hcphotography.co.uk
Thanks for making a ball pool to represent happy times!

Thank you ball pool kids and adults: Beth, Emily, Dan, Sebastian and Monty.
Thanks to Richard Penfold and Jumpinevents.co.uk for the balls.

If you want your kid to thrive in modern life –
and you can't find the answer on Google

The Handbook for 21st Century Mums and Dads

More happiness - less stress

Felicity Evans

Published by
Filament Publishing Ltd
16 Croydon Road, Beddington, Croydon,
Surrey, CR0 4PA, United Kingdom.
Telephone +44 (0)20 8688 2598
www.filamentpublishing.com

The right of Felicity Evans to be recognised as the author of this work has been asserted by her in accordance with the Designs and Copyright Act 1988.

Illustrator: Millie Townsend

Disclaimer: This book is for educational and informational purposes only, to suggest choices. It should not be considered medical, legal or financial advice. It is not a replacement for professional diagnosis, medication, or therapy.

ISBN 978-1-911425-19-9

Printed by CreateSpace.

Contents

How do I come to be writing a handbook for you as a mum or a dad? It's to share with you, as a 21st century parent, about what can work well for your kid to thrive so life is happier and less stressful. Lifestyles are changing rapidly nowadays. We need to open up new paths for our kids.

My awareness about the kids of today developed through being with them on a daily basis, especially at NatureKids.

I got to know the kids very well. I started **Understanding** their behaviours and needs at a very deep level, seeing that heightened sensitivity needed support to be a gift rather than a block. If I wanted children to read, or stop hitting, I found the right **Nurturing** for this to happen. Then kids began to learn easily and be kind. The most challenging usually became the most **Loving** - I still get hugs from them to this day.

I discovered ways to help children with **Communicating** and expressing their feelings. Their speech matured beyond expectation. Kids want **Resolving** to happen - right now - to sort out troubles or distress. Then they can go forward in life with self-worth and confidence - wonderful to see! **Playing** was the way to be their true selves.

Understanding, information and knowledge bring hope. As I see kids finding their own feet in life through the 6 Steps, I experience ever increasing hope for their future and know that others can do the same.

Possibly 65% of children starting school today will be doing careers that we can't imagine. The 10% most popular jobs for young people now didn't exist 10 years ago. Home or school can't really prepare children for these innovations but luckily their brains are ready! Let's have the courage to support these young pioneers in our own homes and as a society.

Many are asking for a lifeline, often vehemently with challenging behaviours or all-pervading anxiety. This can be stressful and utterly exhausting for parents. I encourage you to recharge with some of the suggestions in this book - they can give you a boost in energy and confidence. Then you can hold your patience during any tough times, so they pass much quicker.

When we consciously prepare our kids for life today, things are easier, more relaxed and happy for everyone. As kids thrive in the present, their future is bright.

Introduction
Life is easier as we enable kids' brains to thrive

When I was on teaching practice in Infant school many years ago, the kids used up masses of grey paint! It was the Daleks, first time around. They made Daleks from junk, painted them grey then proudly wrote 'This is my Dalek'.

That's what kids did in infant school in those days. We didn't have photocopiers for worksheets, junk was free and children spent hours making junk models.

I didn't focus on it then but the Daleks highly motivated kids to practise fine motor control, be creative and feel good about an end result. Nowadays neuroscientists would say that they were becoming whole brain children, building the effective brain pathways for learning and adult life.

Years later in 2000, I set up NatureKids. Some kids came because they weren't able to 'mature their brains' and learn in present day regular schooling, others joined us because their parents wanted them to have a different approach to learning.

I got out the junk again but most kids didn't know how to 'do junk'. They chose playing outside, for hours on end. Drew, a helper, noticed they were acting out the archetypes, which American philosopher Joseph Campbell sees as practising skills for adult life.

The children created their own ways to expand their brains and build self worth, sometimes overcoming very marked differences. I offered Understanding, Nurturing, Loving, Communicating, Resolving and Playing - the 6 Steps - in a very simple way but what happened was extremely profound. The kids truly thrived. Their friendships were like blood brothers. They became kind and caring. They sang, danced, drew pictures,

developed beautiful handwriting, read fluently, understood maths and wrote stories from their hearts.

It's now about three generations since schools did 'junk modelling' or similar for hours on end. Unsupervised outdoor play happens less and less. Many adults haven't had whole brain schooling or whole brain opportunities at home. This can make life very stressful for them. But our brains have neuroplasticity throughout our lives. There are simple strategies for life to be less stressful and much happier. This handbook isn't about turning back the clock, it's about offering easier, effective ways to live today, both for you and your kid. If your kid is resisting learning or life in some way, be proud. They actually want to get back to using all of their brains and heal up any suffering from previous generations, to be competent adults in the future.

I am very interested in neuroscience now but this book originates from how I naturally started to support kids, from my teens, before I had any scientific knowledge, so it is a quick and easy read. I have put links to neuroscientists if you want to look up the facts.

I have written about the reality of life as it is for a very wide range of children and families. It covers many aspects of family life from 'taking time to blow bubbles', to phone bullying and Coercive Control. All is written without judgement, instead giving suggestions and solutions.

Through this handbook I am offering to be a personal PA to make life easier for you, so you can enable your kid to fully thrive.

www.drdavidhamilton.com
www.drdanielsiegel.com
"Follow your bliss." *Joseph Campbell* **www.jfc.org**

From Heartache to Happiness

Heartache is losing yourself

When adults are struggling with any aspect of life, at work or at home, we call it stress. When children are finding aspects of life difficult, whether for brief moments or long term, we call it many things from being naughty or uncooperative to being

oppositional, defiant or avoiding demands. We may not even notice the distress of an anxious or withdrawn child sitting at the back of the class. Kids call all this heartache. Their stress is not only in their thoughts, it pervades their whole being, but they feel it most in their heart. Some painfully draw broken hearts. Many wishfully draw beautiful hearts. They make hearts with Hama beads to hold onto for their own comfort, or to share their love with others.

Some kids will act out heartache: like Ollie throwing his homework on the floor and refusing to do it; Polly holding tightly onto my hand everyday in the Infant playground; Katie crying that she just hasn't got a 'listening Dad'; Kenny trashing the room because it's too much for him to get in the car to go swimming.

If things are tiring, stressful, challenging or just don't seem quite right with your child, explore what might be causing their heartache. They might be being bullied, or feeling a sense of failure. It might be that their brains are wired up for their 21st Century life and they are struggling to adapt to conventional education or previous family patterns.

Some will hide heartache. For a few, there might be dramatic examples of this, like self-harm. For others heartache is transient, like the death of a pet. It works best to encourage kids to express heartache rather than bottle it up and put on a neutral or brave face, as it has to surface in some way sooner or later.

Heartache can be feeling frightened, lonely, lost and disconnected, for a few hours, or a lifetime. We can help kids move through their stress and distress, their heartache, with the 6 Steps in this book.

Happiness is finding yourself

Happiness is Ollie being able to do his homework easily; Polly happily giving me a gift years later when she confidently left primary school; Katie being completely absorbed playing on the trampoline with friends; Kenny calmly turning to me and saying he loves me as he runs around the maze.

Happiness is recovering from the death of a pet - ideally children can build up resilience to naturally move through sadness and loss.

Happiness is building self-identity and enjoying being oneself. It's being able to communicate feelings and receiving support for any traumas, regaining good physical and mental health.

When life is going easily for you with your kid, you see their happiness and joy.

Happiness is feeling well, full of vitality, courageous, creative, connected, caring and at one with others - community.

Inspiration from Harry Thompson

On the next page is an excerpt from Harry's autobiography, aged 9, and a recent email. He writes about his intense anxiety as a small boy, causing him extreme heartache. This was not recognised or supported. Throughout much of his school life he was seen as naughty, lazy and defiant. He saw himself as stupid, despite being highly intelligent. At 14 his Asperger's type of behaviour and communication was picked up, but for him this focused on what he couldn't do, rather than who he was. After some very traumatic and self-destructive years, I recognised his Pathological Demand Avoidance patterns when he was 18. This tied in with who he felt he was, and he began to manage his differences by learning the 6 Steps for himself, revealing profound inner talents and gifts.

The recent email shows him thriving and being himself as an adult. He shares this as he wants all children to have the freedom to be themselves, and has written his autobiography *Sensory Overload Robs Me of My Moral Code* for this purpose. It is being published in 2017.

Harry's journey from Heartache to Happiness

Harry writing about his childhood anxiety, aged 9:

Around this period I was overbearingly clingy with my mother and acutely paranoid about just about everything. I had daily panic attacks because I thought that she would never be there to pick me up from school because she'd be dead or something else horrific. One of my classrooms overlooked the school playground where all the parents would gather every afternoon to pick their sons up. I spent the remaining hour of school with an unwavering gaze at the playground, tentatively awaiting the arrival of my mother. Sometimes my teacher would grab hold of my head and turn it so I was facing the front of the classroom. I can vividly remember how stiff my neck was and how hard she had to pull my head to break my gaze.

Everything was too much for me. My mum would play Pavarotti in the car on the way to the school to help calm me down. I loved classical music so much, I still do in fact, but listening to Nessun Dorma or Caruso was the perfect thing to appease my nerves in those dreaded mornings before school.

1st November 2016, email from Harry:

Wow yes! Mirror-touch synaesthesia is incredibly interesting! It's good that we now have science behind our crystalline sensitivity and empathy.

Travels are going well. My book is very nearly complete, I just need to save up some money to pay off the editor. She has one more half of the book to do.

On that note I am actually working right now and living 100% independently! How you may ask? Well I've actually acquired myself two PDA (Pathological Demand Avoidance) friendly jobs. One is a self-employed food deliverer and the other is a self-employed English tutor. I teach children in China English from home via Skype. It is so rewarding to finally be able to earn income whilst being myself and utilising and honing my skills.

I am living with friends in Southern California for now. I have a lot of projects I'm working on. I am going to start YouTube blogging with a friend. We are going to record/film us having a conversation on what it's like to be sensitive in a multisensory world. We will discuss politics as well, and we will talk about how schools can be reformed and how more emphasis should be placed on the cultivation of creativity and not just on regurgitating arcane mundane academic trivia. I will keep you posted!

Speak soon, Harry

The Handbook for 21st Century Mums and Dads

I have written this handbook to offer you the type of support that I give to parents when they contact me. I can't be a friendly voice on the end of a phone to you but I can let you know that I understand how it is for you.

My aim is to offer you support and compassion via this book. My website, www.felicityevans.co.uk, is there to share articles and links to other sites with parents in similar circumstances.

This book is written for mums and dads of children aged about 4–11 but you can change the activities and language to suit your child's age.

Take your time to read and absorb the suggestions in the 6 Steps. Just think about one idea at a time and be patient with yourself and your kid.

Twenty-first Century kids are growing up in different ways to previous generations. When this is working for them, life flows easily and harmoniously.

Anything else is a child's attempt to get back to being themselves.

So all kids experience heartache at times: a pet dies; they get their sums wrong; they fall out with a friend. We may not identify different types of heartache when our child presents as uncooperative, aggressive, defiant, moany or huffy. If you are getting irritated or to the end of your tether, step back and think 'heartache'. What can I do about heartache?

This book is written using 'your kid' but some parents may have more than one. The idea is to look at each child individually in order to most lovingly blend them into the family group.

This book is also for adoptive parents, carers, grandparents, older siblings, teachers and anyone who spends time with children.

This handbook is not just to read - it is something you do

This book is written with one important phrase on each page.

Most of the pages are short so the points are quick to read.

Sometimes the page is only a couple of sentences. These are little gifts to you, maybe giving you an 'OK', 'Got that!' or a nudge to help things get easier.

Occasionally some points are more detailed and carry on over two pages. This is to give you a clearer picture of the message, more to ponder on and a real feeling for the information.

Make these ideas and strategies your own. Some may like to jot down ideas in a list or journal. On some pages there are links to books or sites for further information. These are in no way essential for this book to work for you but just there if you want to look at certain subjects in greater detail.

We can help our kids build a strong sense of self and move through heartache into happiness, with:

Understanding, Nurturing, Loving, Communicating, Resolving and Playing.

As we do this, it updates family patterns and brings our parenting in line with 21st Century needs. Once you have read a few pages to understand some of my terminology, you may like to just flick through a few pages anywhere in the book and choose a page to enrich your day with your kid.

Read on to fully enjoy being a 21st Century mum, dad, carer, friend, teacher...

Understanding

'Isn't it nice how well they get on together, despite being so different.'

Understanding

Introduction

Children are born with an inner knowing about who they are, and they expect parents and the other adults around them to be aware of this knowing or wisdom. They expect to be fully understood, and anything else can hurt their feelings, sometimes very profoundly.

Parents focus is usually on how to make learning easier for their children, from walking and talking to good qualifications, because that was the path offered to them.

There is a big difference between inner knowing and acquired knowledge.

Kids first want to develop their inner knowing and to be recognised, understood and loved for who they are. This section offers insights into a deeper understanding of your kid.

Most parents aim for a good day with their kids, every day. But kids nowadays are very different from how they used to be. If your reference for being a parent comes from your own childhood, it may not work, even if childhood was easy for you. For many, childhood may not have been a pleasant or easy time, and so it's even more frustrating when you are doing your very best to make it happy for your kid.

Lack of information about the kids of today, added to the various stresses of present everyday life, can prevent a good day. Then it can be a struggle to face the day.

The more you wish for your kid to be a bit easier to manage, to co-operate more, to play more contentedly, and, let's face it, some days just be more easy to love and be with, the harder work they seem to become. And your vows to stay patient, calm and collected can dissolve before breakfast. You may seem to be getting to the end of your tether more often than not.

Parents of today need quick, easy information to understand why their kids are different from them or other kids, innovative ways to manage these differences, effective strategies to structure the day. Your kid is determined to be themselves and life is easier when you facilitate this.

Then they build self worth, wellbeing and resilience, and life becomes so much easier for the whole family.

Understanding Contents

Understanding 'Owls and Cats'

Understanding Struggles or Gifts

Understanding Sensitivity

Understanding Pioneers

Understanding Owls and Cats

Explore, play, learn, communicate, love and be loved

All kids want to **explore, play, learn, communicate, love and be loved**.

Yet nowadays many kids may do some or most of these experiences in very different ways to previous generations.

As we explore the ways in which this generation of kids is different, we can start to understand how life works best for them.

Then not only do we help them, but we reap wonderful rewards from being with them.

Let's open up a variety of possibilities to help our children thrive, develop and mature into their true selves.

Let's generalise two different types/characteristics of kids on the next few pages, to focus on how to best communicate and be with them, both in words and actions.

Understanding Owls and Cats

Positive and purposeful strategies

Some kids blossom and thrive from when they are little and naturally adapt to our world but nowadays many need a little more understanding and support to manage even everyday life.

When I am out and about I meet lots of mums and dads who have concerns about a child, ranging from slight worry to a very major concern. I encourage parents to persevere and explore what support is available in school or from your GP. Focusing on your kid's challenges extends general understanding of our kids today – many are different! This is an important part of evolution.

There is also much that parents themselves can do in everyday life with their children.

This book gives mums and dads **positive and purposeful strategies** for the kids of today. These kids are of their generation and some previous strategies

from professionals or teachers aren't working for them. This isn't your child failing – this is them wanting to be true to themselves so they can thrive and give the best of themselves to the world.

The innovative ideas on these pages will give practical ideas that you can immediately put into place. Then even the most challenging or withdrawn kids can grow from struggling to thriving.

The suggestions here will work for most kids even those diagnosed with named or labelled difficulties, as these only a small part of the whole child. Whatever label a child has, you can support them being their true selves, which makes life so much easier for them and for you.

By recognising the differences of kids today, our kids can experience them as gifts rather than hindrances.

At my website **www.felicityevans.co.uk** you can read about others solving similar dilemmas. You can also ask for further ideas.

Understanding Owls and Cats

Watchers/Feelers

More kids are being born as **'watcher/feelers'** nowadays - let's call them 'Owls'. As babies, many do the stare into your eyes; they like you to hold their gaze and respond with a smile!

These kids quietly watch what is going on, picking up what others are feeling rather than look at what they are doing.

They sum up people and situations and need time before joining in. They live in their emotions and feelings, but may internalise them and not express what is going on inside them. They expect you to know!

They need familiarity to feel OK before they step into their day, and will withdraw when they stop feeling OK.

Owls may experience life very differently to previous generations. They are highly aware and sensitive and may need support to manage everyday life, or they can retreat into their own worlds.

Picture an owl, still, silent, with wide open eyes, taking everything in. When they capture their prey, they are furtive, keeping it to themselves. Owl kids will be similar with achievements, probably enjoying them on their own, in their own way, in their own time. We say 'wise owl' and often these kids have a knowing or wisdom, even if they don't initially show it, or those around them don't recognise it. This can be painful for them, as they feel misunderstood or not recognised. They may not talk much, as non-verbal communication is far more important for them. They take everything in and ponder on life. Owl kids can be quite solitary and may even feel lonely, so we can help them to feel connected to what is going on around them, the family and life in general.

Check that they feel integrated in school, that they can learn easily, and are not just following everyone else. Many may go through the motions of school without fully understanding concepts and this may make learning and school more and more stressful. They may tell you how their teacher is feeling. If they feel a teacher is stressed or depressed, they may resist going to school because they can't handle people who are not feeling OK. They experience others' feelings to such a huge extent and often can't override this feeling - they will expect you to know that, as it's the norm for them.

An owl kid can't understand why adults are not paying attention to their own and others' feelings, and aiming to feel happy.

Understanding Owls and Cats

Speaker/Doers

Other kids are '**speaker/doers**' -
let's call them 'Cats'. These kids are
constantly chatting and doing, often
wanting attention.

They are more interested in what
others are doing rather than how they
are feeling, and join in quickly if they
like the look of the activity. They need
a favourite or very novel idea to start
their day. If an activity isn't going well,
they can create a drama, crisis
or fuss.

Sometimes the activity is to avoid
how they and those around them are
feeling, and they need encouragement
to express their feelings appropriately.
They may externalize their sad, angry
or scared feelings with behaviours until
they learn effective ways to manage
these feelings.

Cats may seem more similar to
previous generations in the way they
talk, play and behave, so it is more
puzzling when they resist everyday life.
Nowadays, Cats also have heightened
awareness and sensitivity and may need
support in conforming to everyday life.

Picture a kitten in full play, alert
and active, leaping and pouncing.
They quickly change from playing
to meowing for supper, eager to
get your attention, then purring
with contentment once they feel
relaxed. When they capture prey,
they come bounding to show you,
meowing loudly. Cat kids want to
show you their achievements and
to be acknowledged. Kittens enjoy

the moment, as do Cat kids. Cat kids are verbal and overtly communicate with people. Kittens play together, though usually one is dominant - this can be more of a problem with kids! Play is all-absorbing and they won't want to stop. Find an interesting activity when a change is needed for a Cat kid, and use relaxing stories for falling asleep easily.

Check that school is experiential for Cat kids. They want to prepare for adult life by playing and talking. Kittens don't do worksheets as preparation for catching mice!

A Cat kid can't understand why any adult is not aiming for a very active, fun day.

Understanding Owls and Cats

Opposite Owl/Cat type to your kid

Owls like you to help them manage their feelings first and foremost, especially in the morning. When they are feeling happy, they are ready to do the day. Cats like to do something that makes them feel good to start their day and to have a continuation of feel-good activities throughout the day. Then they can do the necessities of life.

If you are an **opposite Owl/Cat type to your kid**, the differences could stress both of you. But with an awareness of this you can establish harmony.

Owl parents and teachers can encourage Cat kids to be active and verbal, without getting too hyper, perhaps with the help of other Cat adults. Check the kids are having fun and feel happy.

If you are a Cat parent or teacher, allow Owl kids to be quiet and ponder, without becoming too withdrawn. Check how you are feeling, and restore yourself to OK if stressed. Build security and confidence in Owl kids.

Check both Owl kids and Cat kids find their passions and come into their power.

Owl/Cat siblings can complement each other's day happily, but some may clash big time! Cat siblings tend to demand more and more interaction from an Owl sibling, and if they don't get it they may feel annoyed. Owl siblings want peace and quiet and prefer to play on their own much of the time, so a Cat sibling may feel unloved. It helps to support them in finding common ground where they can do their own thing first. This usually means giving attention to the Cat kid, while the Owl kid has space. Then they will more likely settle to play together.

All kids need to be Owls sometimes and Cats at other times, so you can practise this with them.

Owls need encouraging out to explore interesting things, with toys, activities, walks in the woods or park.

Cats need moments to assess how they are feeling.

Both need 'teeth cleaning' and chores to be made easy!

Ken Robinson: Ted Talk, RSA Animate: changing education paradigms
The Element - How Finding Your Passion Changes Everything

Understanding Struggles or Gifts

Heightened awareness in another area

If your kid struggles in one area, it is highly likely that they have **heightened awareness in another area**, even to the extent of a special talent or gift.

For example a kid who finds it difficult to read, which is a 2D task, may be especially clever with models or art which are 3D tasks, or gifted with music or singing.

A kid who has impaired hearing may experience music through vibration.

Kids who present as 'shy' may be summing up situations, acutely aware of how others are feeling. Usually they are naturally open-hearted and just need time to be friendly and chatty.

Kids who have delayed speech may have an acute inner awareness of the world and feel more connected to, say, nature than those who talk in a more usual way.

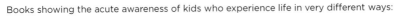

Books showing the acute awareness of kids who experience life in very different ways:

The Reason I Jump by Naoki Higashida.
The Spark by Kristine Barnet.
The Horse Boy and The Long Ride Home by Rupert Isaacson.

Books showing the acute awareness of adults who experience life in very different ways:

Thinking in Pictures (and other books) by Temple Grandin.
A Painful Gift by Christopher Goodchild.

Understanding Struggles or Gifts

Do need a label

Getting the right school and ongoing support can be stressful and take time if your kid does have a difference or difficulty.

Some kids **do need a label** to be fully understood. A label may also help with getting support in school, and sometimes financial support. A diagnosis of something like dyslexia, dyspraxia, ADHD or being on the autistic spectrum may sound negative, but the label is not who your kid is - it is just a part of them. It doesn't need to be a burden to them or an excuse to not manage to the best of their ability.

For parents and family, your child is no different after they get a label than all the times before they had that label. If the label helps you to understand your child better, then that's useful.

Kids with even very marked labels can still blossom and flourish, become delightful and loving, and very often succeed in remarkable ways. Even those who show no conventional success can still hugely enrich our lives with their presence. They can be pioneers and bring about innovative changes in many ways.

As with all kids, what they receive they will give back to us tenfold.

This book is full of suggestions that work to enrich lives of regular kids and their families, but it will also help kids who have a wide range of labels.

Understanding Sensitivity

Prevent sensory overload and feeling overwhelmed

From my observations, most kids are born or are becoming more aware and hypersensitive nowadays. This can make them very vulnerable, even those who appear tough.

They need a huge amount of help to **prevent sensory overload and feeling overwhelmed**, as described throughout this book.

Overload and overwhelm can also come from sudden fears or complete panic. Your kid may fear you are not coming to collect them. Other fears often stem from disapproval, which can result in constant anxiety. Most of their anger stems from sudden fears or a build-up of ongoing fear. Many children experience fear and anger as 'heartache'.

They can't usually explain how they feel at these times so watch out for the negative behaviours that indicate this type of heartache: disturbed sleep patterns; eating problems; excessive withdrawal; constant thumb-sucking, chewing on something or other self-comforting patterns; profound weeping; attention seeking; rudeness; screaming; swearing; kicking, hitting or biting; breaking toys or other things; meltdowns; repeatedly continuing to do what you've asked them not to do; not complying with requests; being stroppy and grumpy.

Ensure your kid feels heard and understood by working through the suggestions in this book.

Let's lessen their overload! The 6 sections in this book create 6 different ways to do this. All are important to form a whole, and to bring about wellbeing and happiness.

Understanding Sensitivity

Swimming and sensitivity

An example of how some kids have struggles with life can be shown by looking at **swimming and sensitivity.** Lots of children absolutely love going swimming, a few hate it, but for some it causes them an inner turmoil. They really enjoy swimming but subconsciously dread the sensory overload:

- Noise: joyous shouting, echoes, whistles, splashing, loud music

- Smell of chlorine

- Chlorine hurting their eyes

- Sun or lights hurting their eyes, directly or glinting on water

- Pool water going in their nose, ears or mouth, or over their head

- Hearing other people being told off, usually with very loud voices

- Having to remember rules

- Finding it difficult to hear instructions, or follow them, especially in a cap

- Being unable to copy what they are being shown

- Frustration when they physically want to do something that they can't manage yet

- Finding it OK to be wet in the water, but uncomfortable getting out

- Being embarrassed to be seen in just trunks or swimsuit

- Getting tired with all the above, plus swimming or playing in the water

- Enjoying it so much that it is really difficult to want to come out.

Some can't remember that they absolutely love swimming - they instinctively remember the sensory overload and then they are reluctant to go. So ease the journey with a distraction like a comic ready in the car. Observe what seems to be causing the most overload, remembering that this is a neurological issue not a kid being fussy. Chat with them about what might help.

When kids have to get out of the pool, have a warm towel ready. Bring up their blood sugar with a protein snack before they even get dressed and have water to drink as being in water increases thirst. Use jokes to entertain kids while they get dressed! It's good for kids to learn to swim, for safety and pleasure.

Understanding Sensitivity

Support to come out of survival mode

Some kids need careful **support to come out of survival mode.** Neuroscience is starting to understand how many kids experience our world, with differences like extreme sensitivity to smell or heightened hearing - sometimes to the extent of misophonia. Others see things differently, as with eidetic vision, where they superimpose imaginary things onto what they can actually see. Some sense others' pains or feelings as if they are their own - mirror-touch synaesthesia.

What feels normal to you may cause them to feel overloaded and overwhelmed in everyday circumstances. The heightened sensitivity can help them develop increased awareness which can be a gift later on in life if they manage to find ways to cope with it and feel happy being themselves.

Check if your kid shows signs of sensory overload. Loud noises can be a very common overload, but it can be smells, bright or flashing lights, textures and tastes of food, the touch of certain fabrics or clothes labels.

Kids can especially be overwhelmed by their feelings: fear, anger, grief; and the feelings of those around them. Focus first on your own feelings and wellbeing. As with the safety instructions on a plane, 'put on your own oxygen mask first'.

Your child may be using every ounce of energy every second to just manage, or maybe you can see that they can't manage.

This doesn't leave any energy or time for pleasing you or others, even though they may be desperate to do this.

---

www.misophonia.com Feeling distress from sounds like a ticking clock, someone's breathing.

www.dictionary.com/browse/eidetic-memory Visual recall as clear as something happening now.

www.braindecoder.com/post/mirror-touch-synesthesia-1125428974

Due to be published in 2017, Harry Thompson's autobiography *Sensory Overload Robs Me of My Moral Code* describes what extreme overload and overwhelm feels like. Harry writes very honestly and openly, so more kids are understood. Some of his feelings and behaviours may match your circumstances. His teenage years are a particularly challenging read.

Understanding Sensitivity

Kids are sponges to others' feelings

Kids are sponges to others' feelings. When you have small transient emotion in you, like a burst of anger, a wave of grief, a flash of fear, the effects of this can become deep, deep-seated in your kid because they haven't yet built up the inner resilience to return to feeling OK. The feeling can stay in their awareness for their whole day, for weeks, months or years, and block their development, learning and maturation.

This is probably one of the most important things to consider about the kids of today, to help them come through heartache to happiness.

Kids have been explaining the sensation of mirror-touch synaesthesia (MTS) to me without knowing the name. This is feeling what is happening to someone else, as if it is inside oneself. If we understand that they feel what we are feeling, it makes life easier for them and MTS can be useful rather than stressful.

The emphasis has changed from what we do with our kids to who we are being, and especially how we are feeling alongside them.

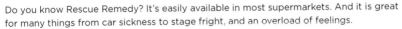

Do you know Rescue Remedy? It's easily available in most supermarkets. And it is great for many things from car sickness to stage fright, and an overload of feelings.

Kids also love Indigo Essences. There are combinations for Sleep, Fear, Confidence, Settling, Chilling. These essences also help overload and overwhelm. www.indigoessences.com.

www.nhs.uk/Conditions/synaesthesia/Pages/Introduction.aspx

www.mumsnet.com/Talk/behaviour_development/a1176256-Synesthesia

www.braindecoder.com/post/mirror-touch-synesthesia-1125428974

Understanding Sensitivity

Lessen the anxiety

Heightened sensitivity can lead to very purposeful pursuits or work in adult life, but as sensitivity, awareness and intuition develop, there is often an increase in anxiety, as the two go together. Anxiety is usually neurological, as with a retained Moro or Fear Paralysis Reflex. So steps need to be put in place to **lessen the anxiety**, internally and externally, by maturing the Moro or Fear Paralysis Reflex and gently supporting the circumstances that trigger it. Anxiety can lead to a build-up of distress, huge heartache and anger.

An example of heightened sensitivity may be when a kid refuses to go to playgroup or school. Sometimes this is linked to insecurity, not wanting to leave home or their main caring adult, but also it can be linked to how a peer or adult is treating them.

Older kids can explain that when their friend's pet died, for example, not only do they feel sad about the pet but they feel the other kid's grief as well.

This is different to empathy - knowing and understanding how their friend feels. They feel their friend's sadness as if it was their own. So they don't want to be with their friend as the feelings are too much for them to manage.

Likewise, an adult or teacher may have had a shock or be unwell and the kid feels this, as if they had had the shock or they are unwell themselves. This is a bit like seeing someone else being seasick causing you to feel seasick. We don't want to dull sensitivity or heightened awareness as it is a gift, but we can give children the inner tools to manage both that and the anxiety, as described in the following Steps.

The Highly Sensitive Child by Elaine Aron.

To mature reflexes: Neuro-developmental therapy. See Bob Allen's questionnaire on **www.felicityevans.co.uk**, and the Fear Paralysis Reflex Checklist and information.

Understanding Sensitivity

Kids have their own agenda

Kids have their own agenda. This isn't selfish or naughty - they are being aware, honest and starting to learn self-responsibility. They are expressing that things are OK, or not OK, for them. They want your love and trust and to feel connected and safe.

When you ask them to do or not do things, it usually feels to them that you are asking them on your own account.

Bring it back to them. Chat about what they are feeling and experiencing, rather than what you want. If your child doesn't want to clean their teeth, does it hurt or feel uncomfortable? Or is it because they are busy playing or don't want to go to bed? Get a softer toothbrush, different toothpaste, take the toothbrush to them rather than interrupt play, and make bedtime very pleasurable.

With, say, homework, pleasing the teacher or working hard to get a good job later in life may mean nothing to children. They are in the moment, and there is life to be getting on with rather than homework. This is an opportunity for you to be there for your kid, talking about how they are feeling, fostering deep trust, rather than them experiencing you taking the teacher's side.

Maybe enable your child to get homework done very quickly, or make it more engaging for them. Talk to their teacher if homework is a struggle. It should just be a quick reinforcement of what has been learnt in the lesson rather than trying to learn something they haven't managed in the lesson. Most parents aren't school teachers so they shouldn't be expected to teach for academic achievement.

Living to their own agenda is how kids are trying to understand life and practising how to manage, a crucial part of growing up.

To explore neurological reasons for homework stress, see 'Mum of the Moment' at **www.felicityevans.co.uk**

Understanding Pioneers

Happy and successful adults

Check if your child's school sees the children who concentrate and find reading easy as being good and successful, and the ones who hop around and can't read as 'naughty' and 'unsuccessful'. Both of these attitudes can lead to stress and heartache, increase a tendency towards obsessive behaviours and even lead to long-term damage as the focus is on what your kid is doing, rather than who they are.

Happy and successful adults are often the ones who never sat still as they were developing a wide range of skills before reading.

In the UK we ask kids to learn academic skills like reading much earlier than most countries - sometimes three years earlier. Many are just not ready, especially those with summer birthdays. They can be disadvantaged for life. If your child isn't ready for school at four, you can legally keep them at home and Home Educate them, short or long-term. You can also withdraw a child from school if it continues to distress them and if they seem to manage better in a quiet home environment. It's not how long a child has in school that leads to success; it's how they manage learning and life.

Kids who find academic tasks easy may need encouragement to explore their inner strengths and talents.

All kids benefit from developing inner resources of self-worth, resilience and an awareness of their true selves.

Neuro-developmental therapy can support kids who are struggling in school. See Bob Allen's questionnaire on **www.felicityevans.co.uk**

www.home-education.org.uk

Educating Ruby by Bill Lucas and Guy Claxton.

www.charactereducation.co A headteacher's advice on developing good character.

www.jubileecentre.ac.uk/1635/character-education Character curriculum in schools.

Understanding Pioneers

A pioneer

Encourage your kid to be curious and allow them the time to explore.

Initially this may be a twig, a hole or a stone, then imaginative play, often acting out the archetypes - the typical patterns of human behaviour - with other kids.

Many teens nowadays are fascinated by exploring the very deepest aspects of life.

Your kid may want to be **a pioneer.**

Explorers in the olden days travelled to explore the world. Kids nowadays tend to go on inner journeys, to explore their thoughts, feelings, beliefs, attitudes and what interests them about the world, people and life.

This can start quite young, and may give you challenges!

Children tend not to want to 'follow on in family footsteps' and may be quite rebellious or withdraw if they can't do rebellion.

They are changing the family blueprint to update it to one that will work for their generation.

From their hearts, kids want to love our very core, not what we present to the world.

Given freedom and support, the right people and circumstances, they are bringing about amazing changes.

This is a very positive part of evolution.

Useful essences similar to the popular Rescue Remedy provide helpful support for children who want to overcome their fears and challenges, and to be kind and loving: www.indigoessences.com

Understanding Pioneers

Changes

Some kids struggle with **changes** from a different T-shirt to transferring classes, especially if they'll have a new teacher.

Your child may need a lot of support to cope with changes, so practise them in a gentle way.

Check how you feel about changes, especially those that take place in your kid as they mature.

We need to encourage our kids to manage change - this builds the inner resilience needed for everyday life.

For kids and adults change can feel like losing their sandcastle as the tide comes in. But we can swap our focus to enjoying the waves splashing on the sand and the chance to create a new castle once the tide goes out. Letting go of the old sandcastle renews our energy to build the new one. This may be letting go of what you want, of specific outcomes. Knowing that leaves space for yourself and your child to create something new, the very best for both of you. Many who have experienced deep trauma can do this.

Life improves.

Thinking of the sandcastle, we are not losing something, we are re-forming the sand. If our kids are struggling, we can re-form their lives so they can cope and thrive.

Have courage, and restore your inner resources along the way.

---

www.carlrosierjones.com The Caveman Principles help everyone deal with everyday stress and change.

www.actionforhappiness.org Support and groups for a happier and more caring world.

www.henryfraser.org Henry showed immense courage when he was paralysed aged 17 and had to rebuild his life.

Understanding Pioneers

Don't want to grow up

Some kids **don't want to grow up**, like the story of Peter Pan.

Part of them may stay neurologically young, so if your kid retains very young behaviours, watch out for this and seek support.

It's fine to cuddle up like a baby at times, even when you are eight, but if young behaviours are happening a lot outside the home and with peers, it indicates a deep-rooted need. It can also cause kids to get teased.

Children will mature through many stages of development, so be ready to let go of the young stages and enjoy being with them as they develop - this eases the 'terrible twos' and the 'tempestuous teens'!

Neuro-developmental therapy can help kids mature. See Bob Allen's questionnaire on **www.felicityevans.co.uk**

Understanding Pioneers

Value your kid

Value your kid for their love.

Look out for their strengths and gifts, as they may not be obvious.

Explore these as your main priority.

Alongside this, be aware of difficulties and seek further understanding, support and compassion to solve these.

Value your kid for who they truly are.

Nurturing Part 1

'That was a quick and effective
move you made.'

Nurturing

Introduction

Nurturing is what we naturally do, when nothing else is getting in the way.

Nurturing is what you do to be a caring parent, with your child's best interests at heart.

The usual nurture of food, shelter and love has stopped being sufficient to bring kids from survival mode into security and maturation for a few generations and, generalising, we have ended up in a society full of poor self-worth, anxiety and depression.

The brain has neuroplasticity, so if we start with that and how we function neurologically, we build inner resilience, self-worth, good wellbeing and happiness. We do this a tiny step at a time, by changing our daily life patterns, how we talk to others and the thoughts that we have inside our heads. Initially this may be a bit tricky as probably it's not what we have been taught in school or at home, but soon it becomes empowering and fun. We create our lives by what we think, feel do and say. Kids love this approach to life!

There is a vast amount written about nurturing our bodies and brains. Whereas kids used to have basic foods and play out, nowadays we do need to look into nutrition, fresh air, exercise, play and friendship.

We can ask our schools to increase nurture by using the ideas in this book and the suggested resources, as they are proven to support the best academic standards.

Approach the Nurturing section with an awareness of Cat or Owl differences in your kid.

---

www.felicityevans.co.uk

For schools to support wellbeing:
Educating Ruby by Bill Lucas and Guy Claxton.

www.charactereducation.co A headteacher's advice on developing good character.

www.jubileecentre.ac.uk/1635/character-education Character curriculum in schools.

Nurturing Part 1 Contents

Nurturing the kids of today

Nurturing with Words

Nurturing the kids of today

Nurture

Check how your kid is experiencing **nurture**. Ask 'How do you like to be loved?' If they are not feeling nurtured, they will display heartache through negative words, actions or behaviours, illnesses or a delay in development.

It's not so long ago that parents were concerned about their child surviving physically, and this is still the case in some areas of our world. But nowadays many parents are more likely to be preoccupied with their children's behaviours, learning and emotional state, or they may even worry about the wide range of mental health issues.

The suggestions on the following pages can bring about positive behaviours, good learning and happiness. There are ideas for very specific nurture for kids' brains, bodies, minds and spirits; for vitality, self-worth, resilience and good relationships, to enable them to fully become themselves. This is building complete wellbeing, leading to strong mental health.

Some children need external support for the usual family nurture to work, and there are links for this on some

pages. In the past, nearby extended families gave a range of support to the nuclear family. Without this and with lifestyles today, family life can be brimful of daily stress.

To counteract this stress, the most effective additional nurture is to look at the root causes of health and other issues. In some areas there are Functional Medicine GPs who work in this way to benefit the whole family. Likewise there are the homeopathic hospitals. It's worth looking at the range of complementary therapies to see what might suit your child. The ones suggested in this book have been used by families for many years, usually with excellent results. If you do take your kid to a therapist, always make the suggestion to your kid in a way that makes it a good experience, by saying that it will help them with the positive aspects of their life: their football, their singing, their drawing, their friendships.

Avoid drawing attention to what isn't working well, or giving them labels of what might be 'wrong' with them. Brain differences can be a gift! So if a label is needed for understanding, support and compassion, or financial support, outline the positive traits rather than the problems.

Ensure you are 'putting on your own oxygen mask first' as they say on planes, and check your own nurture and wellbeing. Otherwise your kid may pick up on your heartache, however much support you provide for them.

Think about how an Owl Kid or a Cat Kid would like to be nurtured.

See **www.felicityevans.co.uk** to support your own wellbeing and that of your kid.

www.functionalmedicine.org GPs who look at the root causes of all problems.

www.vantullekenbrothers.com The doctor who gave up drugs.

www.actionforhappiness.org

www.homeopathyeurope.org

www.bcma.co.uk The British Complementary Medicine Association.

Nurturing the kids of today

Confusion between nurture and control

Most kids feel a **confusion between nurture and control**, as do most adults, and it helps to get this really clear in your mind.

For some five-year-olds holding your hand near a busy road feels like control, even when you are doing it as nurture. They will show this by struggling to escape from your hand. It is best to pre-empt this and similar situations with a preliminary pep-talk, at a quiet and calm moment. Gradually introduce the following thoughts to a small child: 'You are starting to grow out of your jeans. I can see you are getting bigger. Soon you will be old enough to stand carefully beside me without holding my hand when we cross the road. For now you can just hold my finger tightly. I would love to see you stopping carefully at the kerb, looking both ways for cars, and listening to see if you can hear a car. Can you show me this next time we go out? Then you can practise safety by telling me when it looks OK to cross.'

Always role model safe ways of doing things to your child, naturally and easily, as this is what they will copy.

The same philosophy of checking that your sons and daughters experience nurture rather than control applies in many situations, even after they leave home! The earlier that this becomes a joint discussion and agreement the easier life is for everyone.

So with 'limiting nurture' that is making a demand on them to do or not do something, make it very special and pleasant for them, a time when your child can feel responsible, co-operative and proud. Of course keep to safe measures for their age and ability.

Nurturing the kids of today

If your kids wants a puppy, don't get them a goldfish

If your kids wants a puppy, don't get them a goldfish.

Kids of today are very different from previous generations: they are more aware, sensitive and vulnerable, even when they present as self-sufficient or tough. It can be tricky to help them feel well and happy and to meet their needs. They crave a puppy, a cookie monster or a skateboard and are upset when this doesn't solve their problems and make life happy.

It may not be practical or possible to get them a puppy. Children can be demanding but you will notice that even if you can get them everything they want, this doesn't make them happier. External gifts don't heal inner heartache.

Instead you can focus on removing any heartache, reducing as much stress as possible and meeting their deepest needs to build inner resilience. Talking to even a young child about this helps: 'That girl with the new play people on TV looks really happy, doesn't she? I can see that you want some of those toys. You think they will make you feel better - happy like the little girl. I would like you to feel happy. Can we play a game and spend time together?'

This enables your kid to get back in touch with the core of themselves which is loving, giving, creative and full of light and joy.

When they reach this inner state, they come from wanting and needing all the time to 'managing without the puppy' which makes life truly easier for you. Yet funnily enough, the 'puppy' then often comes into their life in an unexpected way!

Nurturing the kids of today

Used to follow more in their typical family footsteps

Kids **used to follow more in their typical family footsteps.** This could be in aptitudes and study, adult work, interests, ways of being, personality and even wearing similar types of clothes!

This rarely happens nowadays! Kids can be very individualistic from babies, knowing their own minds and exactly what they want, throughout their childhood.

Your child may need support in accepting traditional nurture and it is good to be flexible about what is in their best interests, rather than just using previous patterns of, say, discipline.

Likewise new types of people and circumstances may be stressing them out, and they then need careful guidance and support.

What may seem OK, normal and appropriate, even beneficial to an adult, can be terrifying to a child and cause them a lot of heartache - this will show in negative behaviours or poor health.

For many kids there is a strong inner pioneer instinct, and it is an honour to have a son or daughter like this. Even if challenging at times!

Children are bringing about more effective ways to manage and enjoy life, though this may be masked by difficulties when they are young. The difficulties or differences are the very patterns that lead to new ways of moving out of heartache and towards living our lives more happily and effectively.

A Boy Made of Blocks is a novel by Keith Stuart, but it is based on his experiences with his son. It is such a pleasure to read, and 'Alex', the dad, spontaneously goes on a similar journey to my 6 Steps, with very interesting outcomes.

Nurturing the kids of today

Heal the family tree

We inherit talents such as being musical or creative, practical, innovative or thoughtful. This might give rise to a quality in your kid that gives them a way of life, whereas for you it was a hobby. But we also inherit challenges, such as being fearful, angry, controlling, dyslexic or prone to addictions. These can be heightened in a kid to the extent that they cannot manage life, home or school.

Don't panic or feel ashamed! This usually indicates that the challenge is surfacing in order to be nurtured! This is such a special time to share with your kid, as it will enrich your life along the way: healing fears, anger and control; discovering ways for easy reading; creating wellbeing and resilience that remove tendencies for overuse of phones, working all hours, gambling, smoking, drugs or alcohol.

Our kids are vehemently wanting us to **heal the family tree**, often over several generations.

Nurturing the kids of today

Two family trees

A kid always has **'two family trees'**, one from each parent.

Children may have a residue of hidden, yet very powerful, internal feelings and traits, inherited from either parent. Some of these may be useful for a child, some may be holding back purposeful development. Then they need encouragement and support to surface, sort out and express these feelings and traits.

A usual one may be a tendency to patterns like feeling heightened fear or anger; needing to be in control; not being able to learn, study or work; overworking or over-studying, as well as future possible misuse of alcohol or drugs. These patterns may cover a very wide range of behaviours, including eating disorders and the repetitive traits of autism and phobias.

This applies even when they don't live with one parent or don't have much contact with them. Generalising, when a child is with a parent on a daily basis, they become very familiar with these circumstances and show if they are managing and thriving by their general communication and behaviour. If they

are feeling any type of heartache, this will show. If they don't see one parent very much, this parent can become idealised or rejected.

Similarly, kids may miss useful qualities from a parent they don't see. A typical one that kids miss out on is structure and grounding from a parent who is not in their daily life. The parent with whom they live can check what might be missing and do their best to include that in their kid's daily life or regular routine.

Your son or daughter is half from each parent, and all children function best when there is harmony between parents, whether they live in the same house or different ones. It is especially important to value aspects of your kid that come from an absent parent. You can provide a quality that they may be missing by not seeing one parent so much, from spontaneity to artistic qualities; to routine, structure and being grounded; to freedom and courage. Likewise notice and appreciate when your child shows positive qualities that have come from you.

Especially avoid linking anything that troubles you about your kid to the absent parent. When necessary, seek help in supporting any worrying aspects about your kid, and put as many ideas as possible from this book into place. Have courage and move forward, even if it is just a tiny step at a time. Negative difficulties can be transformed into delightful differences and amazing experiences!

If difficulties are denied, this leads to them getting worse. This can negatively affect a whole family to a very great extent.

If difficulties are accepted and supported, this usually leads to an improvement in wellbeing, health and happiness for all the family.

Nurturing the kids of today

When your kid is gaming/watching TV they still need you

One huge difference with kids of today is their gaming/TV watching. Parents often dismiss this as 'screen time' and think it doesn't have a lot of real value. Some just see it as a time to soothe kids and keep them quiet. But when you devalue your kid's choices about how to spend their free time, THEY can feel devalued.

When your kid is gaming/watching TV they still need you, even though they may look content without your attention.

You don't have to enjoy gaming yourself to value the enjoyment your child gets from a game. So ask if you can watch while they play. Observe the speed of their reactions, how they multitask, their ability to navigate 3D space, their joy as their strategy works and how determined and focused they are. Comment on their choice of activity as you would if it were drawing or building with Lego. You don't need to do this every time, but often enough for them to feel you are being present with them.

If you don't live with your kid, creative online games can be a great way to 'be' with them and to develop mutual interests. This is sometimes easier for kids than 'chatting'. It also gives a quick, familiar and easy topic of conversation when you do see them. Sometimes with young children you can use examples of online courage, and enjoying adventures, to boost their confidence in everyday life. If a kid is struggling at school or at home in some way, they usually turn to a computer. Nowadays it's the way that many kids are finding their way into the world. For some it takes them deeper into isolation, but as a Mum or Dad you can join them in their screen explorations and eventually this will spill over into their actual experiences in the real world – it can give you and your kid a close bond.

If gaming/watching TV is taking up most of their free time, then get them a manual about their favourite programme, find them colouring pages of the characters, maybe cut out relevant pictures and collect them in a scrap book, find the theme tune and play it in the house... balance their use of media by expanding on their interest rather than dismissing it.

This reduces the possibility of screen time becoming obsessive and problematic and results in it being proactive and enjoyable.

A *Boy Made of Blocks* by Keith Stuart – a novel but based on true experiences with a computer game.

Nurturing the kids of today

Watch out for jealousy

Watch out for jealousy. Life isn't always fair, and it's important to build security and happiness for kids to cope with this.

When a kid is showing marked jealousy, it is a sign that they have heartache: a lot of inner tension, anxiety, anger, fear or grief. This is very often linked to family patterns.

Avoid doing 'anything for a quiet life'. This will not solve the problem, even in the short term. It will exacerbate it.

Look for ways to resolve tension and anxiety. Very often physical exertion will help this, especially jumping! Then exercise could be followed by a lavender bath and a quiet time, to encourage relaxation.

Let out anger, fear or grief as explained in the Communicating section of this book.

Build security and self-worth with good pre-empting and lots of appreciation.

Solving jealousy with your kid is very rewarding.

Sitting Still like a Frog by Eline Snel, book with a CD: mindfulness for kids.

Stubbornness

Stubbornness in children always stems from heartache because there is an innate desire to love and please.

If the heartache is transient, the reason for stubbornness is usually identifiable. A classic one may be suddenly refusing to go to school - in which case something there has given them heartache: bullying, falling out with a friend, disapproval over a piece of work, losing confidence with a teacher. Maybe your kid can say what the problem is, or you may have to guess. They will want you to take immediate action so they can go back to feeling OK.

If stubbornness persists, use the 6 Steps in this book to work out the cause and solution.

A few children have such deep heartache that 'stubbornness' pervades every moment of their daily life. This may be a neurological pattern, like Pathological Demand Avoidance (PDA), that needs ongoing support.

Some professionals see this as 'naughtiness' but it is not. Likewise they may not offer compassionate understanding or effective support.

But I have seen so many kids with PDA become their delightful selves, usually very philanthropic and intelligent. Some children were supported with just the strategies in this book and some had the additional help of the listed sources of support.

See checklist for PDA on **www.felicityevans.co.uk**

www.unschoolingaspies.blogspot.com An Avenue Mum blogging the differences.

Understanding Pathological Demand Avoidance Syndrome by Phil Christie, Margaret Duncan, Ruth Fiddler, Zara Healy.

Nurturing with Words

Practise pre-empting

Practise pre-empting. A bit like driving a car, some people naturally take to the pre-empting a parent needs to use. Other mums and dads need a lot more practice. Pre-empting daily occurrences is not taught in most schools, yet! Fixed outcomes and specific answers are usually required in school. Kids do not fit this pattern - they require flexibility, freedom, creativity and ingenuity. If this feels daunting, read on through this book - it will help, hugely. Everyone can do pre-empting in the end.

Pre-empting is closely observing your kid and thinking through their day: love, meals, activities, exercise, community, chores and sleep. If there is a bit of a challenge coming up, how can you support them? Work out how you can ease your kid through their whole day, making it as pleasant as possible for you both.

Some kids who have, say, enjoyed swimming, can't recall that feeling of enjoyment the next time you suggest going. Give them verbal feedback as they are enjoying something and help them remember it later, until their pre-empting becomes easier for them.

Likewise some adults don't see the full picture of something, whether small like presenting a meal differently, or huge like moving house. Certain brain types intently see a small part of the bigger picture - this is a useful gift in some jobs. So check if you have carefully taken everything into consideration with regards to your kid's day and life. Most children need the whole picture to be fully explained then prefer it to be exactly as explained, which is sometimes tricky so be ready to discuss and reassure. Once they know the full picture, they also need the day to work well for them to feel secure.

Becoming efficient at pre-empting is one of the most useful skills for a parent.

Mindset by Carol Dweck, exploring fixed and growth mindsets.

Nurturing with Words

Change the situation

If your kid isn't coping in a situation, **change the situation** rather than tell your kid off. Pre-empt and prepare more for a similar situation next time.

Nurturing with Words

Respond rather than react

It works best to **respond rather than react.**

If you react vehemently, like the 'OW!' when a baby pulls your hair, this can become a fun thing to do because babies and young kids like predictable outcomes! So reactions tend to lead to the words or actions being repeated. If your kid, say, swears and you respond with a loud, 'Don't you dare say those words in this house', they may quite like your dramatic response and go for it many times.

Calm yourself first, regardless of whatever they have said or done. Some kids can cope with a discussion and co-operate easily. Others may initially need an interesting diversion: 'I wonder how many times you can blow out this candle in 30 seconds', to take their focus off what you don't want. With younger children you may not even need to correct or stop them saying or doing what nearly caused you to react in the first place, as something else has taken its place. With older ones you can have the discussion a little later.

If you do need to use correction, calm, clear guidance usually works best.

Nurturing with Words

Give the most attention to what is in your kid's best interests

Avoid swearing or certain behaviours becoming a big issue. Many children like dramatic effects and may do or say things for attention. **Give the most attention to what is in your kid's best interests.** Young kids just love the sound of swear words without understanding what they mean. Then there is an interim period when they start to explore meaning and may become fixated on certain words for a while. They are trying to make sense of adult words and exclamations.

In quiet moments, chat with your kid about life today, and how words are used differently now to previous generations. Explain that they will hear, say, many 'interesting' swear words in different places and online. Their peers will use a very wide range of expletives. Ask them what words they feel OK about hearing, and chat with them about what words you like to hear around the house. Teach them about the appropriate use of language to match what others will be comfortable with. Avoid a conflict of standards.

Maybe make it fun to have exclamations that are acceptable in different places.

Explain that using swearing as an aggressive attack towards someone is unkind and unacceptable. The same applies to insults and teasing with words or actions.

Insolence and rudeness usually stem from a child feeling distressed, unhappy and full of heartache. It's their way of letting out this distress or giving a cry for help. Gently seek and ease the causes of distress.

Many children don't understand banter, yet will repeat what they hear. Again they need calm, supportive help in understanding what's appropriate.

Encourage exploring interesting words and vocabulary, as this helps children to communicate with a wide range of people in different ways, helping them to feel accepted and to bond with a wider 'family'.

Nurturing with Words

Gentle guidance and support

Talking gently with your kid, at eye level, in quiet focused moments, can enable them to be doing and saying what is reasonable for their age, understanding and ability.

If boundaries are controlling, rigid or dogmatic, this hugely distresses all children. Instead discuss information to help them feel safe and secure, like who they can ask for help if they get lost, checking if a branch on a tree is strong enough to take their weight, or running forward as far as the bus stop so you can catch up with them. Then you can trust how your kid behaves, speaks and experiences life, giving them the freedom to be themselves.

Kids need constant **gentle guidance and support** to manage their day in the best way for themselves and others. If you yourself did not receive this as a child, your kid's brain may not be fine-wired for a happy purposeful day. But the brain has neuroplasticity and this can be learnt and practised together.

It works best to discuss with your child what you expect of them in advance, rather than tell them off when they have got it wrong.

Pave the way for them with confident information and requests: 'We can choose the new shoes you need nice and calmly, then we will have time to go look around the charity shop and you might like to buy something small there.' Always explain this matter of factly as a natural action/natural consequence, rather than a reward, which increases stress in a kid. They worry that they won't succeed in what they are meant to be doing. Make sure the good things happen whenever possible or children feel distressed and punished.

Think how certain daily activities feel to them. Many tasks, even mealtimes, can feel boring and even stressful.

Have suitable activities and distractions ready for your kid wherever you are, whatever is going on, especially out and about. This can be little things like comics, finger puppets, sketch boards, joke books and if you can handle it, skill games that make noises! Make the time you stop to chat to a friend very easy for your child. If it isn't, encourage them to say 'I can't be patient at the moment' and change track to interesting them until they are settled.

www.virtuesproject.com A useful list of words to help your child express themselves, like patient, flexible, forgiving.

www.charactereducation.co A headteacher's advice on developing good character.

No-Drama Discipline by Daniel Siegel and Tina Payne Bryson.

Nurturing with Words

Make it easy for them

If your kid is struggling with getting thoughts, actions and behaviours right, **make it easy for them**.

If they are throwing balls at windows, other kids or you, swap the balls for soft beanbags or put them away until you have given them the maturity, security and self-regulation to throw balls appropriately and enjoyably. You can explain that you are waiting for them to be old enough to play safely with balls. Encourage power games where they can win.

Aim to support them to come off the computer as appropriate, healthy, and best for their wellbeing. Avoid nagging and battles. Perhaps ask them when their video or level will end and suggest that as a good time to do another fun activity. Show respect for their choice of activity. Ideally your kid will create a balance in their daily activities all by themselves, like doing a physical activity after being on the computer, but some need gentle guidance and fun ideas.

Gradually aim for it to be easy for your kid to manage coming off the computer to do other activities. Tell them what you feel about the level of their use. Explain that you enjoy their company and doing interesting things with them. Talk about what works for you as well as them and come to a win/win solution. Agree suitable times and remind them of this agreement. Be kind, caring and firm.

Consciously give them pleasant and interesting thoughts throughout the day, so their minds don't fill up with anxiety, old traumas or inappropriate, stressful subjects.

Encourage activity and creativity and give them frequent and obvious reassurance and clear feedback. Acknowledge when things are easy for everyone.

Nurturing with Words

Allow change to come

If things don't seem to be going as well as you would hope with how your kid is developing, being, talking or behaving, seek the root causes and set about sorting them out.

Then chat to your kid about what behaviours might be purposeful and positive for them. Have an open, positive and confident mindset that change can happen for your child and you. **Allow change to come**. Then you are no longer victim to negative behaviours.

Practise all the ideas in this book. They will work!

Felicity's website with support, information and articles for parents, adults, teens and kids: **wwwfelicityevans.co.uk**

www.naet.com For allergies, intolerances, to eliminate toxins and enable better absorption of nutrients.

www.cease-therapy.com A homeopathic programme to help autistic kids, but also good for other symptoms and stresses.

bob@accesspotential.net for neuro-developmental therapy.
There's an informative questionnaire from Bob Allen on **www.felicityevans.co.uk**

The Whole-Brain Child by Daniel Siegel and Tina Payne Bryson.

Nurturing with Words

Avoid the two Js: Judgement and Justification

Avoid the two Js: Judgement and Justification. Kids can feel in a split second when they are being judged from quite a young age. Judgement takes away security and self-worth. It can lead to meltdowns, withdrawing or hiding away, or even running away.

Not judging your kid doesn't mean leaving them to do or say what is inappropriate or wrong.

Instead of judging, which has strong elements of disapproval, discuss in a quiet and calm moment what is appropriate and purposeful behaviour. Aim to enable your kid to find life easier, rather than be annoyed or cross when they are struggling.

Words like 'Don't climb too high or it makes me nervous', are justifying something from your point of view. Kids may not feel heard or understood about their desire to climb high, and react accordingly.

If you experience something as inappropriate or wrong, have a calm chat about your feelings and discuss alternatives.

If you have reacted with sudden anger, honesty does work: 'That gave me a shock. I am sorry I shouted at you. I am calm again now.'

Nurturing with Words

Pre-empt and enable

It is always best to **pre-empt and enable** your kid to do what you want in the first place.

'Those bumps you are so enjoying on the platform are there for a very special reason. They are to help blind people know that they are near the edge of the platform, to keep safe as fast trains whizz by. If you walk on those bumps, that will be very confusing for blind people. They may stand too close to the track for safety. Can you see the grid on that gulley for the water to go through? That could be your train track. It is safe. What about seeing if you can be a train going along that track?'

'Get off those bumps. You are too near the edge of the platform and that's very dangerous,' means very little to a kid fascinated by walking on bumps.

Maybe you would have just got off the bumps as a child when asked. Parents have to be a lot more creative and inventive nowadays! This is all part of children knowing their own minds earlier, exploring the world as intently as they can. Be very proud and encourage this exploration, intelligence and determination.

Nurturing Part 2

'Yummy!'

Nurturing Part 2 Contents

Nuturing the Body and Brain

Made up of the food and drinks we put into them

Our bodies and brains are **made up of the food and drinks we put into them**, as well as our thoughts.

Health and wellbeing may be dependent on what your kid eats and drinks.

Many kids have allergies and intolerances to foods nowadays, especially the staple foods that most people eat. But these can be lessened by improving your kid's diet and exploring the natural ways as listed in this book.

Sugar, even in natural or dried fruit, colourings, preservatives and additives may well make your kid more overactive.

Foods affect children in different ways. What may be very beneficial for one child may give another tummy ache. Things like wheat and gluten can be difficult for some kids to digest. Dairy may be increasing mucous and respiratory disorders. This can be explored by your doctor and complementary therapists.

Sometimes the side effects of medication or vaccinations can cause problems for your kid, so this can be reviewed.

Foods and drinks can affect your kid's health, sleep, moods, learning and behaviour, as well as their physical health. The best foods for your kid can improve all of these - sometimes dramatically! Always consult your doctor for major problems. There is lots of good information about nutrition and general health and wellbeing.

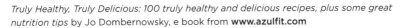

Truly Healthy, Truly Delicious: 100 truly healthy and delicious recipes, plus some great nutrition tips by Jo Dombernowsky, e book from **www.azulfit.com**

Everyday Superfood by Jamie Oliver.

Raw Magic by Kate Magic.

Hemsley and Hemsley: The Art of Eating Well by Jasmine and Melissa Hemsley.

www.naet.com For allergies, intolerances, to eliminate toxins, absorb nutrients.

www.cease-therapy.com A homeopathic programme to help autistic kids and other symptoms.

Nuturing the Body and Brain

Natural ways

Natural ways of bringing up a kid work best for the kids of today. They are being exposed to so many more toxins and stresses than previous generations - in their environment, their circumstances and their foods.

Rather than feel overwhelmed by this fact, there are simple things to do to lessen a child's overload.

We can nourish our kids - body, mind and spirit.

There are many resources for studying the best nutrition for your kid. The most important aspect is to find food that your child really likes and looks forward to eating. If there are a lot of processed, refined starch and sugary foods around, kids may well crave these and nag for more and more. If they have fresh foods, fruit and vegetables as their norm, they will enjoy these. A family approach where kids are involved in the planning and cooking makes it easier for kids to make sensible food choices.

One idea is to keep their food intake as near to 2/3 alkaline foods (vegetables, fruits, seeds and safe nuts) to 1/3 acidic foods (starches, meat and fish). Some kids digest food more easily with their starches and proteins at separate meals. A wide variety of fresh foods is important.

Aiming for a healthy gut is probably one of the best ways to improve our health, energy, vitality, wellbeing, emotional stability and to have a clear brain. This is especially important for kids during their formative years.

In focusing on our kid's health and wellbeing, we can reap enormous benefits for ourselves.

www.imperfectlynatural.com

www.felicityevans.co.uk See my website for information on nutrition.

www.naturopathy-uk.com

Nurturing the Body and Brain

Obesity

Obesity is on the increase with our kids of today. Some absorb the food before the nutrients are broken down in a way that can fully nourish the body, so there is always a feeling of wanting more. Kids can also crave foods to which they have an allergy or intolerance.

Obesity can lead to major health problems and hugely reduce self-worth, so it is best sorted as young as possible without a kid getting any hang-ups about their weight or looks. Over-eating can often be linked to heartache, from minor to major, and this can nearly always be remedied with many of the strategies in this book. There can be a genetic disposition towards obesity so some kids can have both genetic and circumstantial triggers at home or school.

Many kids start to comfort eat quite young, so sort out all heartache. This is exacerbated when kids are given sweets, crisps or any food as a treat or to keep them quiet in a supermarket. There are plenty of non-food treats and it is better to use these rather than wire up the brain to associating food with feeling okay - food is for when you are hungry.

There are many physical reasons for kids to crave more food than necessary. These range from allergies, to low blood sugar, to the Moro fight or flight reflex, or the freeze Fear Paralysis reflex constantly being triggered neurologically. All these cause addictive eating patterns.

Nuturing the Body and Brain

Lessen obesity

A varied, healthy eating plan during childhood can **lessen obesity** and build good health and wellbeing that lasts a lifetime.

From birth, some kids may not like food, even breast milk. This is different from those who have difficulty in sucking which is often linked to a poor rooting reflex (this can be improved).

Some just don't feel good after eating. This is usually linked to digestive disorders, allergies, or problems like reflux. This can last for years.

Instead of feeling full and contented, they feel uncomfortable or empty. This makes them feel anxious and a vicious circle develops, where the eating causes stress and the stress exacerbates digestive and other problems.

To help a kid who has a poor appetite or finds eating stressful, it works best to sort out the internal health issues and create the most relaxing mealtimes possible. Anxiety often soars in a kid when they have to stop playing and start to eat because the play that was helping them to feel calm and happy is replaced by something that feels unpleasant, even traumatic, to them.

Kids are very varied in what reduces this stress or trauma. Some like to be creative with food by chopping it up or making a face with their food on a plate. This may make others completely refuse their food. Some may need distracting with a story or even TV or a DVD. Some may have periods when they need to carry on with their play. Ask if they would like you to pop the food into their mouth as they are playing. Children will grow through these phases so long as they feel well. Choose whatever works best for your kid to remain calm and happy while they eat. Then the tricky eating times for them are more likely to pass quickly without becoming ingrained patterns.

Nuturing the Body and Brain

Healthy eating is important for happiness

Avoid battles linked to eating as this can escalate difficulties. When a child is anxious, distressed or full of heartache, they may have to win to feel OK. Some are 'fighting for survival' and if they focus on food as their major control, this can have dire results.

Anorexia is massively on the increase, with much younger kids being affected. Kids can often be radicalized into anorexia by their peers, as for some it is an easy way to feel a sense of community, to be one of the gang. The causes usually have an element of physical disorder, communication difficulties and heartache. If the root causes are explored and helped, it can lead to positive outcomes, rather than a lifelong struggle.

Resolving heartache, building wellbeing and establishing **healthy eating is important for happiness.**

www.fixers.org.uk Young people using their past to innovate their futures.

www.felicityevans.uk Information and resources for nutrition.

www.naturopathy-uk.com

Nuturing the Body and Brain

Overcome depression

The number of kids taking anti-depressants showed a 50% increase in five years. But kids can be helped to **overcome depression**. A depressed kid is definitely experiencing heartache. But taking anti-depressants to overcome depression doesn't necessarily lead to happiness.

Kids don't have the same triggers for depression as adults. They are not made redundant or divorced. But the root causes are the same and can be helped by building wellbeing in the body; supporting neurological differences in the brain; learning strategies to overcome stress and to come back to feeling OK; learning the 7Cs as described in

Educating Ruby: Communication, Confidence, Creativity, Commitment, Co-operation, Collaboration, Craftsmanship, to which I would add Connection, Community and Calm.

Neuroscience gives evidence about how our brain governs our emotions and how we can lessen stress, why some people find life easy and some struggle and how we can best help our kids to flourish.

Focusing on wellbeing, establishing inner resilience and creating our reality by what we feel, think, say and do is a necessary way of life for the kids of today.

---

bob@accesspotential.com For Neuro-developmental Therapy. Also see Bob's questionnaire at www.felicityevans.co.uk

Educating Ruby by Bill Lucas and Guy Claxton.

The Caveman Principles by Carl Rosier Jones. To overcome stress and experience success.

The Whole-Brain Child by Daniel Siegel and Tina Payne Bryson.

www.michaeljames.be

www.johnchristianseminars.com

www.naet.com

Nuturing the Body and Brain

Check on how your kid is listening and seeing

Have a **check on how your kid is listening and seeing.**

We assume that kids hear and see the same way as us but how the brain sees, vision, and how it interprets what is heard may be very different.

Kids often forget what they have been told but sometimes when kids are not following requests or appear to be ignoring what you have explained, they have a 'language processing delay'. Some take in just the first part of sentences, like 'Go upstairs…' and lose the second part 'and bring your school sweatshirt down for me to wash.' So they go upstairs, don't remember why and start playing!

They are not being disobedient or naughty.

Always kneel down to make eye contact with your kid if you want them to take in what you are saying. Start with what you want them to focus on so they get a picture in their mind: 'You remember you got paint on your sweatshirt today?' Wait for them to take this in and acknowledge it. Then add 'Please can you go and fetch it for me'.

If simplifying requests still doesn't work, there are effective ways to support your kid's development of processing language.

See Bob Allen's questionnaire for *Neuro-developmental therapy* and Lauren Savage's essay on *Auditory Processing Delay* on my website **www.felicityevans.co.uk**

bob@accesspotential.net

59

Nuturing the Body and Brain

Vision

Vision, how the brain sees, is different from eyesight which is checked by an optician. You may find that your kid may be able to see well with their eyes but not be able to carry out the 14 vision skills needed for academic tasks, especially reading and handwriting. Clumsiness with hands, falling over more than others or bumping into things may also be signs that some vision skills are not developing.

If you suspect a problem, see the book or specialists below to check and support the important development of the eyes for 2D and 3D tasks. Babies first develop 3D vision and lots of kids need extra input to fully mature their 2D vision for reading and close 2D tasks.

Many more kids nowadays have eidetic vision. They don't imagine pictures in their minds, as most have done in the past. They create moving people and objects imposed over what they can actually see. This imaginary world is all around them, from birth. So if you are expecting your kid to start writing on a blank piece of paper, they may find it very tricky to do this as their paper is 'hidden' by a 3D version of their recent model or the game they have just been playing outside with friends. Their vivid, imaginative games superimpose over the whole room! This can make it almost impossible to settle down to a 2D task. But once their 2D vision matures, with support if necessary, children's eyes can easily move between near and far vision, 2D and 3D tasks. Enhanced 3D vision is a wonderful gift that can last a lifetime and lead to various careers.

Magic Eyes by Leo Angart.

www.babo.co.uk Behavioural optometrists.

Nurturing with Structure and Boundaries

From resistance to co-operation

Sometimes only a small difference is needed to help your kid go **from resistance to co-operation.**

This small difference is usually linked to focusing on understanding what is going on inside them with intuition and an open mindset. Maybe we can't see the wood for the trees and a quick chat with a friend can often help us to see situations in a different way.

One subtle difference is for you to have a small change in attitude: 'My kid wants me to feel well and happy, but they can't possibly see that doing their homework without a struggle would be great for me!'

If you focus on letting your kid see you as well and happy first and foremost, they may do their task more easily, especially if you think of interesting ways to enable them to start.

Maybe join in with a task like homework, or get them to set you a few sums, or write the shopping list alongside them, or look at a magazine. You are there, fully present, but encouraging them to be independent.

Nurturing with Structure and Boundaries

Enable your kid to be helpful

Enable your kid to be helpful, rather than expect it.

Be patient! It may take a while.

Both Owls and Cats will feel it is more important to be loving than helpful. Any request from you (or anyone) may feel to them that you are asking them to be less loving, less creative, less themselves, less innovative.

They want to be the fullness of themselves for you and everyone and the task may make them feel a shadow of themselves, taking them away from feeling loving and being their best for you.

Use choices for your kid: 'Would you like to tidy up now while I wash up, then we will have time to go to the swings? Or shall I help you when I finish, than we will just have time for the supermarket?'

If you role model feeling good while you do chores like tidying up, your kid associates these tasks with feeling OK and they can even find them a pleasure. Make necessities fun and easy from as young as possible.

Nurturing with Structure and Boundaries

Avoid reward and punishment

Make absolutely sure that you **avoid reward and punishment** to get your kid to do what you want.

This is controlling and manipulating and your kid may repeat that back to you. Being controlling and manipulative is very damaging for them and their future.

'Father Christmas won't bring your presents if you are naughty', is opting out of taking responsibility for how your kid is feeling and behaving and putting the responsibility on your kid and Father Christmas. Neither of these ways is effective in the long-term!

In this scenario, if the joy of Father Christmas is linked to the stress of not being worthy, it wires up a confusing and even damaging stress/joy link in the brain. This prevents a child building self-worth. Also if a child has been playing up for some reason (heartache from somewhere) and the presents still arrive, this is giving them an 'I can get away with anything' attitude which doesn't feel good inside them and can be distressing.

Celebrations and festivities can be stressful for a child, so like their other challenging circumstances, deliberately plan to make these times easier and more joyful.

Nurturing with Structure and Boundaries

Punishment/Reward

Punishment usually increases anxiety, fear, anger, despair, negative behaviours and delays maturation and academic progress.

Punishment is saying it is OK for me to distress you but it is not OK for you to distress me or anyone else.

Enable kids to do what you want with gentle nurture, discussion and negotiation. This is something that can build up to last a lifetime.

Waiting for **rewards** increases stress and stops your kid feeling self-worth in the moment.

Waiting for rewards causes anxiety as the waiting seems endless. Kids know that they may not meet the expectations of what they have to do to get the reward and dread failure.

Then often they stop before attaining the expected target.

If you give them the reward anyway, without achieving the expectation, kids feel useless and worthless because they know they failed and they cannot enjoy the reward.

Nurturing with Structure and Boundaries

Spontaneous surprises

Spontaneous surprises are fun and focus your kid on associating feeling good whatever they have to do. It's better than using the offer of a reward to get them through the task in hand that they don't want to do. They then need the reward to feel OK and will start nagging.

It's best to enable them to feel OK as they manage the task, as this builds the internal resilience that they need for life.

Spontaneous interesting and fun surprises enable your kid to experience and feel 'I am getting this right' which gives a big boost in confidence.

Nurturing with Structure and Boundaries

Unpredictable friend in their pocket!

Watch out for your kid - they may suddenly have a very **unpredictable friend…in their pocket!** Mobile phones can be useful and fun - but for some children, even young ones, phones have become a scary part of life that is hard to get away from.

When we are with a person, we are absorbed together and it's less likely that they will change from being friendly and having fun, to suddenly teasing, bullying or threatening - possibly many times in an hour. Yet this is what is happening with phones nowadays. The teasing, bullying and threatening can be hugely more intense than in a playground because the one doing it is at a safe distance. They don't see or take any responsibility for the consequences of their words - these can be completely uninhibited. We need to offer an immediate source of strength and support to those who are being bullied. For those who are bullying we need to focus on special attention to solve the causes of their bullying, followed by ongoing guidance to help them to start being kind. People only bully when they are unhappy or unwell. Everyone can learn the scientific fact that kindness is good for us as it improves our health and our own lives, leading to happiness. 'Happiness is a skill that can be learnt.'

Supporting a kid with keeping safe and secure on their phone is a bit like cleaning teeth - it will affect their wellbeing throughout their life, except with phones it is their mental wellbeing that could be at risk. Regularly notice how your child is feeling while they are on their phone and check for anxiety or withdrawal. With a bit of luck kids will become responsible for cleaning their own teeth! With phones, carry on watching out for children's wellbeing throughout their teens.

When kids have a smartphone, they may have to stay on hyper-alert and be ready for anything. For a few it's like living in a permanent crisis. This can be very damaging.

They may start to display the signs of distress and overuse: poor sleep; high levels of anxiety; being withdrawn, stroppy or rude; spending hours at a time on any sort of device; skipping meals or activities; staying up late; frequently retreating into their room and locking their door. Have a chat and discuss without condemning or shaming. Maybe use this as a teachable moment on how to cope with whatever is going on. Give understanding and supportive feedback. Otherwise you may feel your kid is slipping away from you and the situation escalates. If you are deeply concerned consult the professionals, as they have useful experience and suggestions.

The techniques in this book will help you to communicate effectively with your kid and keep up your support, whatever is going on for them.

'Happiness is a skill that can be learnt,' Shamash Aldini **www.museumofhappiness.org**

Childline: 0800 1111 and **www.childline.org.uk**

www.culturereframed.org/the-crisis

The Five Side Effects of Kindness by Dr David Hamilton

Nurturing with Structure and Boundaries

Thrilling, frightening and moreish

Over the past 10 years I have seen the age at which many kids view inappropriate online material, including pornography, come down from sixteen to twelve to eight-year-olds. It is there in many playgrounds.

It's become like joy-riding: equally **thrilling, frightening and moreish**.

Sexting may be experienced as harmless fun by some children. They want to follow their peers, many of whom will be copying older kids. But as with all phone issues, check they are not being upset or taken advantage of. Don't hesitate to seek professional guidance if you suspect abuse as it can happen in any family. Professionals are seeing the damage phone stress can do and ideally prevention is better than dealing with the after effects.

Taking away children's computers or phones doesn't address their inner needs and is likely to build resentment rather than solutions.

Some schools are building phone and online safety and support with classes of children from eight-years-old. Maybe encourage this in your child's school.

Make it very easy for your kid to get all the support they need.

Being matter of fact works even if you are horrified. Respond rather than react. Then your kid will always feel able to turn to you or maybe accept your suggestions to talk to others, if you feel it is beyond your experience to sort things out sufficiently.

---

www.culturereframed.org/talk-kids-porn

Childline: 0800 1111 and www.childline.org.uk/info-advice/sexting

www.childline.org.uk

www.samaritans.org

Nurturing with Structure and Boundaries

Safe romping, play-fighting and physical play

Safe romping, play-fighting and physical play are very beneficial for kids. They love to be exploring their physical abilities and strength. Just be aware that some kids don't realise that the strength they are testing out on an adult may be too strong when playing with a smaller child. No child likes being physically overpowered or held down, whether by an adult or bigger child. If they are made to feel a victim, they may seek to get their own back, even subconsciously. Chat about what is playful and appropriate and what might hurt too much.

Small children need to win. So if a kid starts to become frustrated, think about fun ways to change from play-fighting to the next activity - maybe developing physical skills.

For example, according to age and dexterity, you can hold their feet and they can walk on their hands like a wheelbarrow. This can be developed to manage with obstacles. You can hold their hands and they can somersault over. They can do a handstand and you can catch their feet.

Be aware that one child may try to verbally outwit a sibling and the other may physically want to be in control. Both of these can be signs of lack of self-identity, self-worth or heartache. If the heartache is addressed, play and communication will become more amenable. There can still be 'goodies and baddies', conflict and resolution, without anyone's feelings or bodies getting hurt. Play is preparation for adult life, so check your kid is heading towards a purposeful future.

Most babies and small kids are naturally very sensuous. They love to explore bodies. Some naturally mature into appropriate actions for their age, some need information, structure and guidance from mums, dads, carers and teachers. This is not to be prudish but to enable a young and vulnerable child to grow into an independent and safe adult.

Affectionate cuddles and hugs remain an important part of childhood.

Nurturing with Structure and Boundaries

Loving structure, enabling your kid to find life easy

Keep to a **loving structure, enabling your kid to find life easy**, so you are less tired, less angry, less frustrated, less annoyed, less worried, less depressed, less despairing, less unwell and have less headaches and heartache. The structure can be discussed with the child, as this develops their understanding and communication skills for the future. Mutually agreed decisions lead towards self-responsibility.

Children can learn action/consequence but check that they don't experience consequences as punishments.

Punishment is something you or anyone imposes on them, like saying they can't watch TV tonight as they were unkind to a friend or didn't tidy their room. It is the responsibility of a parent or adult to enable a young child to be kind and to encourage them to tidy up. With an older child, hopefully they will have naturally developed kindness and their room is probably their responsibility.

A consequence is a follow-on result. If kids are too noisy and disruptive in the car, the consequence is that you need to wait until they are going to be responsible so you can drive safely. Again calm behaviour in a car is the responsibility of the adult but you may need to help kids fully understand the importance of being safe in the car.

Practising safety with your kid not only helps them but you also, as a stressful time changes into a pleasant experience.

Showing and teaching Action/Consequence in a kind and caring way is one of the most important gifts to share with a kid.

This builds inner security and strengths that will last a lifetime.

It builds creativity and enables the brain to see solutions rather than the problem.

No-Drama Discipline by Daniel Siegel and Tina Payne Bryson.

Loving

'This is fun!'

Loving

Introduction

Loving is a state of being our true self, who we naturally are when nothing else is getting in the way.

Love is natural and easy - it just is. It embraces openheartedness, fearlessness, calm, vitality, passion, peacefulness, fun, gentleness, joy, enthusiasm, bliss and smiles.

Yet, our relationships with another person, whether partner or child, family or friend, boss or employee, can be hard work because many people have insufficient practical information to make relationships easy. This book is written for mums, dads and kids but the strategies to improve understanding and communication are helpful for everyone.

So, what gets in the way of love? An unloving act, to oneself or others, is always a cry for help, to get back to being able to love. The kids and young people of today are often crying out for help, sometimes with dramatic and challenging behaviours.

Feeling intense fear, or sudden rage, takes away our ability to love - always - sometimes for a few moments, sometimes for a lifetime because we can't love and fear at the same time. Kids need to experience love. Anxiety and anger cause fixed mindsets as we strive for security and survival. They rob us of creativity and the ability to find solutions. It may feel like others are causing us to feel furious or tense but those states stem from inside us. Usually there are physiological and neurological causes for fear and rage that can't be seen by others.

We see grief as something we can help people to recover from and we don't usually judge grief. Very often something external has happened and we can offer loving and sympathetic support. But we usually judge anger and fear, in children and adults, and disapprove.

This book sets about explaining the causes of fear, anger and grief in children and how to enable them to move through these feelings towards wellbeing, self-worth and inner resilience. When needed, the suggested approaches in this book can improve any internal health issues linked to feeling anxious, stroppy or miserable.

The same type of support can help adults who experience excessive worry, anger or sadness.

Then, as the other 5 Steps in this book - Understanding, Nurturing, Communicating, Resolving and Playing - are established, relationships succeed as love becomes natural and easy. Keep an awareness of whether your kid is predominantly an Owl or Cat type.

This section aims to give you the information for your relationship with your child to be as easy as possible, the most fulfilling and naturally loving.

Children want to love and be loved.

Loving Contents

Loving Yourself

A Loving Childhood

Lovingly Present

Unconditional Loving

Lovingly Safe

Loving Yourself

Let your kid love you

For most mums and dads choosing to have a child gives the opportunity to give love to that child and to maintain this love for ever. Actually, the most important opportunity is to **let your kid love you.**

This has nothing to do with the child's ability to show love to you, whether they are newborn, school age, teens or adults themselves, because loving a parent is an innate desire, even if this takes a lifetime to achieve.

It's about letting a kid fully *be themselves,* naturally loving, caring and kind rather than making them do what you think will make them loving and successful.

It's also about you fully being you: not limited by your work, your relationships, your health, your circumstances, even your schooling or childhood.

Fully being yourself and loving yourself opens your heart so it can receive your kid's love.

www.johnchristianseminars.com
Life skills coach for adults, including online, specialising in overcoming fear and developing self-esteem.

Love is Letting Go of Fear by Gerald G Jampolsky.

Lovingly Yourself

Avoid worrying

Avoid worrying about your kid because this is focusing on what is going wrong rather than what could be going right.

Sometimes their struggles bring them gifts: the dyslexic kid unable to read may be gifted three-dimensionally; a deaf kid may become a professional percussionist; an autistic kid barely able to communicate may write a bestselling book; a very ill kid can be inspirational to others.

When kids don't follow the straightforward pathways, often part of them is delayed while another part starts to flourish.

They feel absolutely wonderful when their true gifts emerge.

So, look for what is in their hearts and focus first on nourishing this, then seek solutions to struggles. Enable a kid to read with 'Magic Eyes' and developmental support, the right reading programme and by improving health and wellbeing. Allow a deaf child to use their enhanced other skills. Watch out for unusual inner talents relating to heightened sensitivities with autistic kids. Encourage the internal strengths of a very poorly child.

Mums and dads can't worry and love at the same time. Choose love.

bob@accesspotential.net
Neuro-developmental therapy. Also see the questionnaire on **www.felicityevans.co.uk.**

Magic Eyes by Leo Angart. This book facilitates reading.

Loving Yourself

We all experience heartache

We all experience heartache. For some it is transient and they soon get back to wellbeing and usual activities. For others it can become pervasive and hinder everyday life. We give it labels like certain aspects of anxiety, fear, depression, mental illness, frustration, anger, addictions and autism. But these usually include the resultant behaviours of heartache. They don't tell us the root causes. Heartache is a very taboo subject. Hence many labels have a negative connotation and can keep us in the loop of heartache and stigma.

We say to our kids, 'I have a cough so we can't go swimming today,' or 'I have a sore toe so I can't jump on the trampoline'. We could also explain, 'I have a bit of heartache today, so I am not going to be doing my best with fun and joy. Let's put on a funny DVD so you can laugh and stay happy. My heartache will pass soon and then we can get back to normal.'

Heartache and distress can also become 'fashionable' as children get older, especially on the internet and with addictions like self-harm. Anorexia can be a way to have a close relationship with peers, to act the part of anorexia really well. Kids may find they fit in at the suicide support group more easily than being creative

and purposeful. Psychologists are reporting that where they saw teenagers in great distress after a recognisable trauma, they now see eight-year-olds who present with the same amount of distress even when there has been no obvious trauma. Let's change these situations.

When children experience huge trauma, maybe the death of a sibling or parent, we owe it to them to prioritise supporting their heartache above everything else, for a long as they need and to return to this support whenever they need it in the long-term.

All children feel others' heartache, from birth onwards, so it feels safer for them if we are open about heartache, our own feelings or their distress, and give it the normality of a cough or a sore toe. Openness about heartache works best if it is a family pattern, from mums, dads and everyone. Honesty builds inner security and helps children to recover and return to feeling loved and loving.

It is truly worth having joy, fun, creativity and love as part of everyday life for this generation.

Loving Yourself

Deep loving and joyousness

Neuroscience can now show where in the brain we are feeling heartache. It can be seen on scans. But our brains have neuroplasticity and they can change and recover, just like someone after a stroke can learn to speak from a different brain area. We can ease our heartache and lessen the effects of whatever name we give it.

We can know, start to understand, believe and experience that the greater our heartache, the more our ability to pendulum over to **deep loving and joyousness**. This is really important for children to observe and learn as they grow towards adulthood.

We can learn to handle heartache in the same way that we can learn to drive a car, to speak a foreign language, to cook dinner. We can try out techniques and find what work for us and practise. We are all like athletes running a race. They reach a moment of exhaustion when they suddenly have to let go and let something deep inside them or something more than themselves, take

over - you see it on their faces and in their stride. For athletes, tennis players and many sports people, it's a learned and well-practised attitude. It makes us feel good to watch them but we can all access this for ourselves.

One way to practise letting go is by doing a 'Handing Over' sheet to recover from heartache and practise thinking about what we want, in whatever way works for you. You can do a 'Gratitude List' of everyday good things or especially about anyone linked to your heartache. 'Handing Over' can be part of everyday life for kids.

If we role-model these or other ways to return to feeling OK to our children, they will pick this up for themselves as it is a very natural feeling for kids.

Openheartedness and feeling good enables us to receive the love our kids want to give us and they can become adept at being loving, kind and caring.

Since the extended family ceased to provide help for young families, groups, books, individual coaching, or websites can be a valuable source of support, as listed at **www.felicityevans.co.uk** See also the 'Handing Over' sheet for adults, and kids too.

A Loving Childhood

'The Feeling Better Plan'

Our kids will suffer heartache themselves and at times like these they need more attention than when they are ill.

If they are familiar with heartache being talked about, it makes it easier for them to manage. You can fully acknowledge the immensity of it and also gently remind them of the times they have come through the tunnel of heartache and out the other side.

All negative behaviours will have an element of heartache, so notice this and support without any hint of punishment or retribution. Otherwise it is internalised and this can have detrimental consequences. Preventing a build-up of heartache will create a foundation for wellbeing.

As children grow up, they will gradually build up a vocabulary of words to express their emotions and then be able to chat about their feelings easily and confidently. For some kids who find this tricky, they can discuss their 'heartache scale', using numbers 1–10. Together you can have **'The Feeling Better Plan'** of ways to start overcoming heartache: jumping, running, activities to do, essences, candles, books to read, jokes to tell, a lavender bath, a box of little surprises. This gives children a feeling of comfort and security.

Some children like the 'Handing Over' and 'Gratitude' lists. You can also use the Sharing and Chatting page on my website for them to express what they would like you to do for them with: Understanding, Nurturing, Loving, Communicating, Resolving, Playing.

These activities are external ways to begin to solve any internal heartache. They work as stepping stones to the actual experience of returning to feeling alright on the inside with an open, loving heart.

See Resources at **www.felicityevans.co.uk**

A Loving Childhood

Overcome immense heartache

If your kid is in school, it is absolutely essential that you let the teacher and others in school know about their heartache straightaway. Tell them the causes if you know what they are, so that your child can be supported. The National Curriculum has taken over much of the time that teachers used for pastoral care and natural nurturing. But you can still ask for the understanding and support your kid needs. A distressed child can't concentrate or learn. There are excellent programmes of support to offer to children in a structured way and neuroscience indicates that this enhances a child's ability to learn.

It is also good to let your kid's teacher know when you are in heartache because that can also deeply affect their school day. Heartache could be such a quick and easily understood generic word in communication. It is normal, and private. You don't have to give reasons.

It is absolutely reasonable to say to a teacher: 'Johnny may not be able to concentrate on his spelling test today. I had a lot of heartache yesterday. He tried to learn his spellings but he just couldn't. We'll have another go when I feel back to normal.'

A wonderful reply would be: 'That's absolutely fine. He can do something else. Let me know when he's managed them.'

If the teacher isn't given information your child may receive disapproval and punishment and that could result in them locking in their feelings and perpetuating a distressing situation.

When children have a strong inner resilience and good support, they can **overcome immense heartache** and be stronger from the challenge.

Educating Ruby by Bill Lucas and Guy Claxton.

www.jubileecentre.ac.uk/1635/character-education Character curriculum in schools.

A Loving Childhood

It's never too late to have a happy childhood

It's never too late to have a happy childhood. Having a child is an opportunity to love the child within you and to encourage that kid to let go of fear, anger, disappointment, grief, frustration and to fully live as a mature, nurturing, loving mum or dad and an effective adult. And also to encourage that kid in you to have some fun!

Your kid may push a lot of buttons to get to the authentic, inner you! But that is how they want to love you - with all their heart.

Childhood can be a very happy time for you and your kid.

A Loving Childhood

An extended family

Many kids used to have **an extended family** to meet their needs for love and support, with lots of family and friends nearby. If they fell out with one member of the family there was someone else nearby to turn to.

This is much less likely nowadays.

It places much more responsibility on a mum or dad.

Check you have plenty of love and support for yourself, then seek out as much extra love and support as possible for your kid, so you can share responsibility and not find things so tiring.

There are some places and groups for you and your kid to share excellent experiences and to be very happy.

If you need short breaks to catch up or recharge, you can use a very good childminder as a surrogate grandparent.

Some teenagers want to become teachers or assistants and they just love having a kid to play with - some will do this on a voluntary basis.

Likewise sometimes parents whose kids have left home are looking for companionship with a young family.

Just ask around for those who have good reputations and check peoples' DBS[1] for safety.

It's good to focus on all the people around us who have love to share.

---

[1]DBS, formerly CRB: People are checked by the Disclosure and Barring Service to see if they are safe to be with kids.

---

www.actionforhappiness.org
Structured groups for people who want to share happiness and support one another.

www.michaeljames.be

www.naturaldads.com Great for mums too.

Lovingly Present

Be totally present

Take an extra 5 minutes to **be totally present** with your kid. Stay quiet and let them just be, until they tell or ask you something. Give them your full attention and focus. Aim to be fully present with them and what they are doing, rather being preoccupied with your own thoughts. Keep this subtle and without invading their personal space. Check if they like you to stay at a distance or to come close, maybe putting a hand on their shoulder. Let them continue whatever they are playing without interrupting their flow. Enjoy rather than judge what they are doing.

Try to look at what they are doing through their eyes. Think about what may be going on inside them. Ponder on their thoughts.

Wonder how they are feeling.

Are they occupied happily or stressed?

Do they need you to show interest or to be given some encouragement?

Do they like you to stay quiet or give them feedback?

Children vary in preferences and this may change according to how they are feeling.

How is your love for them doing at this moment? Is anything getting in the way of you being present for them? Can you feel creativity and love exuding from them?

Being present will make the day easier and happier for you both.

Presence by Patsy Rodenburg. Patsy wrote this for actors but it also applies to families. It focuses on the 3 circles of presence: circle 2 being fully present, circle 1 being withdrawn, and circle 3 being 'over the top'.

Impro by Keith Johnstone. A book for adults about improvising in the moment; useful for being with kids.

Lovingly Present

Fun way to be fully present

A **fun way to be fully present** with your kid is to play improvisational type indoor or outdoor group games. An easy one for any age is the Hot and Cold Clapping Game. It can be played with one kid or with a group of adults and kids. It is extremely beneficial for adults to spend time in the moment!

At its simplest, one person goes outside the door so they can't hear or see. The other person or group chooses an object in the room: obvious, big ones for little kids like a table; smaller, less obvious ones for older kids, like a specific book on a shelf. The person comes back into the room and starts to walk around. As they walk towards the object the group starts to clap, very quietly at first, getting louder as they draw nearer to it and stopping if they walk in a different direction or name a different object. When they are near the object and looking at

it, show they are close with very loud clapping. Then there's a final huge round of applause with cheering as they point to or name the object.

As players get more confident, a more advanced version of the game involves striking a pose with the object or doing an action with it: 'putting on a hat' or 'sitting on a chair'. Finally with practice, it is possible to combine several objects that are in the room and poses that children know. You'll be amazed at what can be achieved! Eventually older children may manage a sequence of four actions: 'sitting under the table, with slippers on, cradling a teddy bear and singing it a lullaby!'

It is a pleasurable activity for both the person who achieves reaching the chosen object or final task and the group who has enabled them to do so.

Lovingly Present

Be fully supportive

There will be days when a beloved grandparent dies, you lose a job or the cat has to be put to sleep.

First seek all the support you need, so you can **be fully supportive** for your kid.

All kids will watch adults intently at these times.

This is an especially important time to share love.

Without denying your feelings or overwhelming your child with your stress, have the courage to see your kid through these times. If they observe you managing the situation, explaining that tears are letting out grief and will pass, this helps them deal not only with the present situation but also with the daily frustrations of their drawing going wrong or their model collapsing or the overload of picking up others' distress.

Love and support go hand in hand.

Lovingly Present

Role model self-regulating feelings back to OK

Role model self-regulating feelings back to OK to your kid.

'That person was driving dangerously and I felt scared for a moment. I'm glad everyone is driving safely now.'

'That big bill was a bit of a shock, so now I want to think about something different. Let's go off to the park and have some fun.'

'I am annoyed that person doesn't understand what I mean. I need to pause and take some deep breaths.'

We 'do' our emotions and we can process them and move through the negative ones as quickly as appropriate, especially any that have been triggered by something a child has said or done, or not done.

We can get back to love.

Lovingly Present

Stick up for your kid

Sometimes others complain about our kids without understanding that they are doing their best. They may be crying or screaming because they have earache or are exhausted. A child who feels overwhelmed may hide under the table - for some that might be a step forward from having a full blown meltdown. Kids repeat things like 'Fat people don't feel the cold,' to make polite conversation and they don't know when it's inappropriate. Another 'rudeness' may be caused by poor hearing or a processing delay which can stop children replying to a question. In extreme cases there are relevant cards to hand out, so you don't have to keep mentioning a difficulty, like autism, in front of the child.

Gently explain the reasons and **stick up for your kid**, even with professionals.

The person complaining may not have realized that they have triggered the words or behaviour from your child in the first place.

Their attitude, tone of voice, how they are feeling, and the words they use can all be triggers for a child.

Often people overreact to children and children can't handle this. It usually makes the situation worse.

Show others how you respond to children and how this enables your own kid to return to the best loving aspects of themselves. Then people can see what works for your child and do likewise with them.

Unconditional Loving

Triggered by many things

Some kids are affected and **triggered by many things** like different accents, as it makes it harder for them to process what is being said. If they are hypersensitive to smell, perfumes can be a big trigger.

If your kid is very sensitive, they may be over-triggered and this makes life a big struggle for them.

They want to be loved and to be loving but instead they become fractious, tense or anxious. It feels like you are walking on eggshells with them all the time.

This is a sign that it would help to look into improving their health and wellbeing. There are suggestions in the Nurturing and Communication sections in this book.

Rather than judgment or correction, they need more love at these times to help them return to feeling secure and OK.

Unconditional Loving

Don't take sides

Some children are triggered into negative behaviours even just by having other kids or siblings around them.

Don't take sides, even if it looks like one kid is the main trigger.

They may just be the catalyst who lets out what the other is feeling.

Go back to how you supervised and supported them as a younger child.

Increase being fully present for each child in turn.

Find a good moment to show each kid love and appreciation.

Think if there is an Owl Kid/ Cat Kid type of falling out and help them.

The Owl Kid may need space while the Cat Kid needs company - value and support these differences.

Gently enable them to manage being together more happily, by suggesting what will work for them, rather than telling them off for what isn't working.

Think about root causes of negative reactions and behaviours, which are usually linked to health or an area of delayed maturation for which your kid may need support.

To support health and wellbeing:

bob@accesspotential.net

www.naet.com

www.cease-therapy.com

Unconditional Loving

You still love them, even when you say 'No'

If you do have to use a No with your kid, check that you immediately return to a normal tone of voice afterwards and be sure that they fully understand that **you still love them, even when you say 'No'**. Be clear and use words like 'I love you but I don't like what you are doing right now'.

'No' usually feels like not being loved to a small child so it's really important for them to experience that we can still love someone, even when we don't like what they are doing or we need to say 'No'. This applies to much in life.

Give examples of when you have to say 'No' to a pet. Check your kid knows that you love your pet first! Then maybe use funny examples like having to say 'No' to a pet trying to get in the washing machine, or weeing on the carpet!

Adult priorities like not having sweets before lunch are meaningless to children so always discuss with them and see if there is a solution rather than just saying 'No'.

Explain that you always love them but sometimes there has to be a 'No' about what they are doing or saying. Enable them to manage this.

Increase reassurance, love and affection after any 'No'.

Unconditional Loving

When everything is calm

If you get really angry with your kid, aim to stop as quickly as possible, apologise for how you spoke or acted and stay neutral. Reflect on the reasons why you maybe got to the end of your tether and think how you could have reacted differently.

Give them space to recover. Find a way to disperse your anger and recharge yourself.

It helps children to experience that reasonable angry, sad and scared feelings are normal and we can pass through them.

Children feel others' anger, sadness and fear so deeply that they need help in understanding what's going on, without being overwhelmed by this. If you keep using a conciliatory 'I'm sorry I got angry', your kid will copy this and not build an awareness of how their words and behaviours affect others.

Get back to normal everyday life as quickly as possible then, **when everything is calm,** show your deepest love and affection.

This role models that love and affection are part of normal, calm life.

Unconditional Loving

Experience your kid's love for you

How do you **experience your kid's love for you?** Generalising an Owl kid's love will feel relaxing and peaceful. Let it gradually pervade through your whole being, filling you with an 'aaah', a gentle bliss as you sigh out any tension. It's like stroking a cat or watching a dolphin. A Cat kid's love may feel vibrant and exciting. It will flash through you in an instant, filling you with a 'wow!' It will be fun, exhilarating and inspiring. It's like jumping off the top board at the pool or creating a wonderful meal.

These feelings are very different and just small parts of love which is boundless. We usually offer just a tiny part of love which feels easy, familiar and safe. We either want to receive what feels recognisable to us or what is missing. But this is setting up conditions for love which kids can't be expected to meet.

We can check that first we establish self-love which takes away our neediness and wanting love from others. It is so important to love ourselves. That leaves us free to broaden the love we thoughtfully give to our kids. Then, with open hearts,

we can happily receive the very special love our children have to share with us.

An Owl kid may scowl or have a tantrum if you offer Cat type love. It may be too much for them to handle. They are not rejecting your love.

If you settle down with Owl type love for a Cat kid, they may not even notice or they'll set about enthusing you with a lively activity. They are not rejecting your love.

It absolutely doesn't work to contrive to offer the type of love that will match your child. This will feel totally false to them and make them go 'arrgh!'

What will work is for you to think about what you love being and doing most. Match the love you create for them to what is easiest for them to receive.

Let's use the analogy of a walk in the woods. A Cat kid will surge ahead until they find the best tree to climb or a camp to create. An Owl kid will want to dawdle and scrape a stick in the earth. If you are a parent with one Owl and one Cat kid, you have to find a balance. Ideally, as you enter the wood, there is a clearing where one can dawdle and one rush around. Then most likely once they feel settled and happy, they will join in with each other's activities and be ready to explore further. Paddling in a stream is usually an instant success for both Owls and Cats!

Loving isn't ever a compromise but it can be skilful. We can seek and encourage a balance of the Owl and Cat types of love without limiting ourselves.

Sometimes love just wells up from nowhere! Magic!

If you are the opposite Owl or Cat type to your kid (or anyone else), use an awareness of these differences. It can be really useful. Look for common ground, like the clearing in the wood which allows for divergent interests to become one or like paddling the stream which is instant success, where you can be yourselves… happy…and joyful…and loving.

Unconditional Loving

Avoid wanting or waiting for your kid to please you

Avoid wanting or waiting for your kid to please you, to show they love you or make you happy.

Kids nowadays don't necessarily associate 'pleasing' with 'being loving'. Previous generations did far more 'pleasing' and 'doing' to show love and to receive love.

Kids just love, however much they get grumpy, annoyed, frustrated, scared or tearful about life. These feelings don't indicate that your kid doesn't love you - children just need to let out their angst. The quicker and more fully they can do this, the easier it is for them to get back to a 'loving being'.

Owl kids may be loving by gazing at you with open eyes and a wide smile. They just like to feel love and enjoy it with you, relaxing in a quiet way, maybe even without talking.

Cat kids may draw you their best picture with 'I love you' scrawled across it or they may play a joke on you. They just love to do fun things with you, to express their love to you.

A loving kid may not co-operate or be easy in order to show they love you. But when they are naturally easy, co-operative and enjoying life in their own way, they are being themselves, feeling and expressing their love.

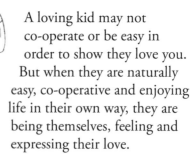

Unconditional Loving

Gratitude and appreciation

Find a moment to show **gratitude and appreciation** to your child for whom they are being rather than what they are achieving. This builds a strong sense of self that can last a lifetime.

'I noticed how kind you were when that little girl fell over. It was sensible to find her Mum.'

'What great concentration you have.'

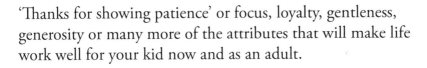

'Thanks for showing patience' or focus, loyalty, gentleness, generosity or many more of the attributes that will make life work well for your kid now and as an adult.

'Thanks for showing me with your face that you are feeling upset. Would you like to tell me about it now or later?'

'Thanks for telling me that you are angry. You have been very clear about what upset you.'

'I saw you having so much fun with your friend.'

Gratitude and appreciation are usually received as love.

Unconditional Loving

Lovingly listen and accept what they say

If your kid talks about fairies and angels or has an invisible friend, just **lovingly listen and accept what they say.**

If you say that these things are not real your kid may feel that part of them is not real. Denying the reality of their experience can make them feel very insecure.

Just check that your child is not becoming withdrawn or obsessive or showing any other signs of not feeling OK. Make sure that they are still being playful, joining in with others and showing signs of happiness and fun.

Lovingly Safe

Safe and OK

If your kid is frightened by zombies, aliens, monsters or ghosts, lovingly reassure them that they are **safe and OK**.

You can tell them that they have a magic finger that they can point at scary things and shrink them so small that they will fit into the palm of their hand. Then things that were scary can be quite interesting, and not threatening.

A child who is in fear can't experience love, maybe for a moment, maybe for a long time.

If your kid remains fearful, seek support as fantasy fear is real for a kid and just as destructive as everyday fears

which also need solving as soon as possible.

Fear is often linked to a retained Fear Paralysis Reflex that causes a child (or anyone) to freeze; or a retained Moro Reflex that creates fight or flight. These retained reflexes can be reduced at any age but as young as possible is best or the anxious patterns can become the norm.

It can also be a sign of higher than usual levels of toxins in the body. Toxins are more easily absorbed when gut health is compromised but this can be improved so good health and wellbeing are established.

www.felicityevans.co.uk See Bob Allen's questionnaire for support with retained reflexes
bob@accesspotential.net

www.naet.com To eliminate toxins and improve health

www.cease-therapy.com

www.carlrosierjones.com For adults to manage fight, flight or freeze.

Lovingly Safe

Delayed gratification

Young children have no idea of **delayed gratification.** They want the new toy, or attention, straightaway.

As they grow older, needing a demand met instantly usually stems from a heightened anxiety, not feeling OK.

Craving a new toy or excessive attention can be a cry for help. It might be an indication that a special love is needed at this time.

First lessen the anxiety, by pondering on any external circumstances that could be worrying a child, by looking into what they might be finding difficult to manage or by thinking about what they might be picking up on with their heightened sensitivity. Then they are more open to receiving love.

Delayed gratification is very hard for lots of children so it might be very tempting for you to give in, to lessen their anguish, screaming, tantrum, or nagging. But if you give in this actually makes them feel more insecure and increases their anxiety. It prevents them from learning a hugely important life skill.

For some kids who continue to struggle, structured practice can help. One way is along the lines of giving them a pound to spend in the pound shop, explaining before you go that this will buy one thing today. If they see more than one thing they like, tell them you will write those items down so they can come back another day soon and choose one more thing from the list.

Give all children time to acquire delayed gratification. Don't make it a long term mission as this may delay the natural maturation.

Coping with delaying gratification can be a very loving thing to establish for your child. It makes life so much easier for them in the end. Kids usually feel proud when they can manage delayed gratification.

Lovingly Safe

Doing anything for a 'quiet life' is not loving

Doing anything for a 'quiet life' is not loving.

It is exactly the opposite.

It is aiming to make a kid feel OK from the outside.

It usually increases challenging behaviours.

It is avoiding the responsibility of teaching your kid how to manage circumstances, feelings and life.

The most loving gift for your kid is to build feeling OK as a strong inner resilience, a foundation for life.

Lovingly Safe

End the day with a good moment

End the day with a good moment for your kid, as a matter of routine.

This can be talking about a happy thought, remembering a nice time in the day or having a big, real heart to heart hug.

So if you have had a tough time, where things for your child or you have got fraught, exhausting, frightening or painful, you have a way to put things on a better track for a good night's sleep and a fresh start for the next day.

Sometimes it's helpful to return to your kid once they are asleep and peaceful, to have a loving thought about them and what's going on in their life.

A kid who goes to sleep feeling loved will awake being loving.

Communicating

*'You persevered well with that homework.
Let's have a bike ride now.'*

Communicating

Introduction

Communication is important, both verbal and non-verbal.

The words that you say to your child are wiring their brain up for their future. How they speak to you is practising for their future.

Non verbal communication includes facial expression, gestures, tone of voice, even attitudes and thoughts which many kids pick up on.

All children communicate from a mixture of what they hear - processing language and what they say - expressing language. Sometimes kids struggle with processing or expressing language and then they can get very agitated. Some may act out distress in dramatic ways, even by not speaking or refusing all verbal demands.

Children want to be heard but if they find it difficult to express their deepest thoughts and feelings with words, they may revert to challenging behaviours or withdrawing.

This generation need to start developing self-responsibility very early in order to thrive in our world today. Involve them in decisions. Ensure they feel heard and understood. Reinforce who they are, chat to them about what is happening around them and help them manage their feelings.

In the past, children had access to long periods of freely playing out with mates to balance out the conformity and learning tasks in school.

Nowadays many kids struggle with school and the language of authority and lack playing out. So it's trickier for them to master expressing themselves creatively, handling their emotions and feeling a deep connection to the family and friends around them. All need to communicate from their heart, the very core of themselves. Academically clever children, 'little professors', are often in their brains, enjoying their ideas and achievements. Yet they still want to be deeply connected to other people, communicating their feelings with a close person.

Coming from the heart is a natural way of communicating and backed up by neuroscientists like Dr David Hamilton and Dr Daniel Siegel and eminent educationalists, like Bill Lucas, Guy Claxton and Geoff Smith.

This is very effective communication for friendship and family, work and leisure.

It can lead to excellent self-worth, happiness and success.

Communicating Contents

Communicating Feelings

Communicating and Behaviour

The best type of words for Communicating

Communicating to Build Security

Communicating Feelings

Talking is not necessarily communication

Talking is not necessarily communication and even young kids may be hiding a lot of heartache. Some children can talk a lot without a parent or other adult having any idea about what is really going on for them.

Cat kids may chat a lot about what they are doing, their ideas and inventions, and not mention their feelings or emotions. Owl kids may mask their stress in life by playing quietly or withdrawing into their own worlds.

The adult language at work, in families and relationships changes over the years but still it's usually from thoughts and knowledge. Children want to share their feelings as well as their thoughts and communicate from the heart as this feels natural to them.

Social media adds massive diversity to our everyday communication. Kids take easily to this. They do best when there is a balance between screen time and free play with friends, outdoors or indoors, when they can play creative games that include a lot of verbal interaction.

Some kids actually have undiagnosed speech and language differences. Some of these kids are seen as low ability but this is not usually the case. They are just having difficulty in, say, building concepts. If offered innovative ways to communicate, starting with the following ideas in this book, children can become very adept at deep, honest communication, especially if their general health and wellbeing are considered.

Children's speech and language can even be delayed by allergies and what they are eating or retained foetal, baby and toddler reflexes and other general health issues.

Mums, dads and children can explore communication together and it will be a very enriching experience for everyone.

GPs can refer for speech and language assessments. Support for language development also from:

www.naet-europe.com.

www.cease-therapy.com.

bob@accesspotential.net See Bob Allen's questionnaire on **www.felicityevans.co.uk**

Communicating Feelings

Kid talk

Many kids use '**kid talk**'. They say something like 'I really hate this house' and you remind them of all the things they like about their house, only for them to scream that they hate the house, or the cat, or you. This can be hard to hear and you want them to feel better about the house, the cat and you. They may not even be able to hear that you love them because this may feel like you're not getting the point. Be patient and loving.

Usually this has nothing to do with the house, the cat or you. Your child is conveying to you that something is not OK for them but they can't put it into words. Likewise they may say 'Can I go out and play football?' If you say No and there is a meltdown, it is not about football.

The meltdown is because they can't say why football is essential 'for their survival'. They may still be picturing the look on the teacher's face when they didn't finish work; or the feeling they had from being teased at playtime. They wanted to

self-regulate back to feeling OK by playing football.

Always show children that you are really listening to them: 'I can hear that you really hate the house'. As soon as football is mentioned, ask 'It looks like football is very important? Can you tell me why?' Ideally they will be able to tell you.

Support what is really going on, without initially aiming for negotiation or discussion. If they are using vehement words they want your support and comfort.

Often it takes a while for a kid to express what is actually going on for them. First help them to relax and once they are settled they will more likely be able to express what they really want to tell you. If you think it is major, aim for this to happen well before bedtime as it may take a while. Otherwise you can have a quick catch-up then: 'What was your worst and best thing today?'

You can use the Sharing and Chatting Activity Sheet on **www.felicityevans.co.uk**

Communicating Feelings

Sad, Mad, Scared, Glad

An activity that may work for well for your kid, whether they are an Owl or a Cat, is for you to draw four big circles on a page for them and then ask them to draw in **Sad, Mad, Scared, Glad** faces. Explain that mad is for anger, not crazy. This simplifies their feelings for them as it gives a choice of four. Some children find it much easier to draw the face of how they are feeling than to put it into words. Watch the face they spend most time drawing, as this will most likely be their dominant feeling of the moment. Another way is to have a 'feeling tree' or coat hanger! Children can make labels of their feelings and hang them on the 'tree'. Sometimes it may be easier for them to find a label than say the words.

You can then give examples of recent experiences for your Sad,

Mad, Scared, Glad. Keep it true and relevant, without dumping your strong emotions on them. So, 'I felt angry for a bit when that person jumped the queue in front of me' rather than 'I felt angry when you wouldn't get dressed.'

Then you can ask your kid to point to the face that best expresses their feeling right now and if they wish, they can explain why they are feeling like this. Some older kids prefer to write down on the back of the page why they have a certain feeling. Younger children may suddenly burst into tears or writhe around on the floor with really strong emotions, even shouting out things like 'I hate

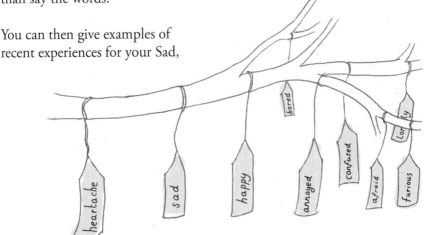

you'. Whether this happens in a structured time like this or spontaneously, they are using a really good way to let out strong emotions. It's brilliant communication, showing exactly what they are feeling. It's not using a negative behaviour, like hitting - that's what they do when they can't let out their anguish with crying or writhing or however they choose. Just calmly sit with them and let them know you are there when they want you. Affirm that it's OK to have strong feelings and it is best to let them out.

Ideally they will become familiar with expressing their feelings to you, whether by words or through the emotion taking them over. Occasionally it may be easier to do the feelings sheet with a different adult. If you know there has been big trauma, like a bereavement or family crisis or a problem for them at school, you can set up play

therapy or professional support. This is something that can be easy, pleasurable and supportive, whatever the crisis. It's the responsibility of the support person to engage your child so you can relax about it. Some kids may be bottling up something that they really want or need to talk about.

It's best not to distract your kid from whatever they are feeling but just to be there for them and if necessary, to help them to process it through, however long that takes. Encourage your kid to let out their angst at home; it's easier than the supermarket. But if it happens in the supermarket, smile at onlookers and say 'It's OK, this angst just needs to come out. We've had a crisis.' Don't let others prevent your kid from expressing themselves - they need to build good health and wellbeing for when they grow into adulthood.

You can use the Sharing and Chatting Activity Sheet on **www.felicityevans.co.uk**

Communicating Feelings

Name the degree of scared, angry or sad feelings

Once kids have an awareness of numbers, using a scale of 1-10 can often help them **name the degree of scared, angry or sad feelings**, with 1 as feeling 'great and at one with the world' and 10 having the most extreme fear, anger or grief.

Kids experience feelings as constant and who they are, rather than a transient moment.

Owls need nurture, support as described in these pages and for everyone else to be feeling good, for them to self-regulate back to OK. After a while they can be encouraged to do activities to help them feel better.

Cats initially need to do something to distract themselves from the feeling to self-regulate back to OK but later can be encouraged to talk about feelings and how to manage them.

When your kid seems to be managing a sad, angry or scared feeling a bit better, ask them what number they are on now. With a smile, acknowledge even going from a 10 to a 9 and reassure them that they are managing their feelings well. With support your kid can soon learn to return to a norm of 1 in everyday circumstances. This is in no way suppressing an emotion, but processing it through.

When you talk about your own feelings with honesty, without dumping them on your child or blaming them, the more it normalises tears, frustrations, fear and anger. This also builds up the vocabulary for kids to express themselves with words.

See the Feeling Better Plan at **www.felicityevans.co.uk**

www.virtuesproject.com This list of virtues can help kids find extra words they need to express themselves, but let them choose which ones they like and match their life.

Communicating Feelings

Express their feelings in an appropriate way

Encourage your kid to **express their feelings in an appropriate way**. Feelings are not naughty or wrong. They just are. If you distract a kid from their feelings, they get bottled up inside. This hugely increases overload and overwhelm. Some may think that letting out feelings distresses a child. It doesn't. They have strong emotions welling up in them that need to be released. If the jug of angst remains full, this diminishes wellbeing.

Young children can't separate out their feelings from another's. Kids in a panic may shout 'I hate you.' Tears frequently follow, then wanting comfort and a cuddle. Expressing their feelings appropriately helps them to learn 'This is just me - the world is still a safe place.'

Adults may experience that others are giving them overwhelming feelings. Some behave in a way that really distresses a child.

We need to make the path to appropriate support for this much easier and without stigma or the situation perpetuates. We all occasionally do or say something that inadvertently upsets a child. We can apologise and help them recover. Let's aim to be happy with our kids.

Often we want our child to cheer up quickly because their suffering is difficult for us to observe. But like a tooth abscess bursting, letting out their inner heartache is a huge relief for them.

Tears are good to let out sadness until your kid can adapt their feelings through discussion.

Really acknowledge fear and let a child cling or stay with you until it subsides. If marked fears remain, seek appropriate support.

Kids can be angry lions, thump a soft settee and scream to let out frustration and anger.

Communicating Feelings

Understand their fear

If your kid is full of fear, ensure you acknowledge it with them and explain that you can **understand their fear**, without increasing their anxiety.

Their fear may be to do with their own lives. But in addition to this most kids pick up on all the news that has extremely worrying content: pollution, cancer, animals becoming extinct, threat and violence. Explain that it's good for people to talk about these things, as it brings about progress and change. Explore with your kid to find what's improving: those who are successful in reducing pollution; less people are dying of cancer because of medical breakthroughs; animals who were in danger are being saved; carrying an alarm keeps you safer from bullies and threats. Compare dangers, like what is less likely to happen than being struck by lightning. Ask if they know anyone who has been struck by

lightning. Bring the likelihood of danger into a realistic perspective. Positively teach how to keep safe when necessary.

Then help them find their courage. Use encouraging words without dismissing their fear. Often it can help to refer to a past experience that they have managed well.

Some kids can feel amazing courage in very dire circumstances, and the same child may struggle with a spider. Fear is fear, and your child may experience overwhelming fear in what to you is easy everyday life.

Communicating Feelings

Fear of everyday things

Lots of kids have **fear of everyday things**, like water. This might be walking on a bridge over water, swimming or even having water put on them, like hair washing.

Water fears can remain for months or years but forcing a kid to do something that terrifies them isn't productive. Water fears, like other fears, can be overcome when the steps are small enough not to panic the child - so think of the tiniest step possible, regardless of what would be expected for kids of that age. It's fine for a child to stay dry at the pool, maybe just start by throwing in small balls to someone, for as long as they need. Don't wonder why your kid is not jumping in at the deep end like some five-year-olds. Value differences. If swimming is forced, it can become a trauma and ongoing fear. Give them plenty of time.

You can enable your child to cope, with complete confidence, whatever the trauma is, or you will find someone else who can if you haven't found your confidence in certain areas like swimming. Just check that what others offer your child brings a smile to their face and that you can really observe their enjoyment. This prevents passing on fears to the next generation, when the fear may be greatly enhanced.

Often the kid most nervous about water can become the one who confidently jumps off the high board into the swimming pool - with gentle support and encouragement rather than any force. Building this type of internal confidence gives children a reference point for talking about and overcoming fears, in order to feel confident in the future.

Communicating Feelings

Classic childhood fears

Another of the **classic childhood fears** in young children is going upstairs, especially when it's dark. You will expect your child to do this straightaway without any hesitation, so it can be very frustrating when they suddenly won't. It might even be embarrassing for you that your child is fearful. But let's look at where the fear stems from: usually it's a vivid imagination, lots of creativity, intelligent thinking and powerful feelings - all things to respect and be proud about. We just need to gradually build up their courage to the level of their imagination.

So, at the top of the stairs, children feel there is the wolf from *Peter and the Wolf*, the gorilla person from the show they recently saw, or someone with a wire to garrotte them from the archaeology film on TV. Even when they are old enough to know this is not true, the feeling of fear is *totally real*. So discussion and rationalisation don't work. Focus on their feeling of fear, rather than the cause they mention. A small child might want to be carried upstairs and for you to stay close by - that's fine, even if that is reverting to patterns from years ago. If your kid is too big to carry, still go

back to the type of support you used when they were younger, maybe by making funny things to do on each step or putting safe, pretty lights up the banisters. Acknowledging the fear in a matter of fact way is not making children more fearful. It is helping them to move through the feeling.

Even confident kids often have fears in school: relating to their work, tests, being bullied, moving up to a new class. Seeing their new teacher tell someone off in the playground could trigger fear about going into a new class. Really notice what they are showing or telling you. Write it down, if that helps them. Discuss and support without pressure for the child to let go of their fear. They need you to stand up for them in school or they despair. They want and need you to take appropriate action for the situation to be easier for them - they are being effective, not difficult. Very often if you ask around, other kids are feeling the same.

Check with words and your full attention to see if your kid is managing to come back to feeling OK. Fear can pass.

Communicating Feelings

Lessen fear

Fear is not a child being fussy or oversensitive. It will often be neurological with the resultant body chemistry, rather than just emotional stress.

They may be in Freeze from the Fear Paralysis reflex or Fight/Flight from the Moro reflex. These reflexes can cause a real panic, a huge trauma.

Kids may have allergies or a build-up of toxins in their body that cause them to feel unwell but they can't understand or explain 'not feeling right'. This often makes them fearful, weepy or angry. If not supported, fear can grow into paranoia, weepy into depression and anger can increase into violence.

Often children and young people cry out for help in ever increasing ways: self-harm, obsessions, addictions, anti-social behaviour. Usually you can't reassure or talk them out of this type of reaction but dealing with the neurological and physiological root causes will always **lessen fear**.

Fear is more likely when kids are tired or overwhelmed, so keep an eye on how they are doing in the day, encourage restful activities and aim to keep overload and overwhelm to a minimum.

Children need practice, vitality and physical wellbeing to express fears and ask for support.

These types of fear are not lack of courage. They are heightened awareness, leading to the type of person who will be a very special adult - the type you would be glad to have as a kind and caring friend or a considerate boss. They enrich our world.

To reduce allergies and toxins and build good health and wellbeing:
www.naet-europe.com

www.cease-therapy.com

bob@accesspotential.net For a programme to move through retained Moro and Fear Paralysis Reflexes.

See Bob's questionnaire at **www.felicityevans.co.uk**

Communicating Feelings

Weep out their tears and sadness

Encourage your kid to **weep out their tears and sadness**. Grief will pass.

Allow them to cry without cheering them up before they have let out their sadness.

Explain that the 'jug of tears' will empty and they can return to feeling OK.

Cuddles usually help for most kids. Ideally they can say if something is making them very sad and you can address the cause.

But some kids can't give the reason and you have to guess. Some may like this made into a game, where you are getting closer and closer to the answer.

If the crying persists or your child remains miserable, just ask your doctor to check that there is no underlying health problem.

Then you can use the same support for an unhappy child as is on the Fear pages. The health and neurological causes can be very similar for grief, fear and anger.

Each time sadness is acknowledged and comfort is given, this can lead towards good health, inner wellbeing and resilience for adult life.

Communicating Feelings

Anger needs to pass

Anger can engulf some kids long term - but **anger needs to pass**.

Encourage them to shout and stamp 'I am feeling very angry because…'. Don't try to change their minds about the situation until the anger has passed.

Offer them appropriate actions like playing angry lions or robots. Kneel down by a soft sofa, mattress or pile of pillows. Hit the soft surfaces as hard as possible and scream loudly for a minute or so until the anger subsides. Sometimes tears follow as the underlying reason for the anger surfaces. Playing with swords or learning sports like karate usually lessens angry patterns of behaviour because it feels good to be powerful in a purposeful way.

It is not OK for kids or adults to take their anger out on anyone else, even if they feel it's someone else's fault. Anger triggers inside us, according to our inner feelings and not what other people do. This is not to say that a child won't be angry with a parent but we want to aim for discussion rather than hitting out or extreme verbal outbursts. If a child is angry with you about something you have said or done, where appropriate, apologise. We can aim to respond, to sort out situations rather than react with more anger.

Always acknowledge that it's good to communicate anger with appropriate words rather than physical aggression.

If you offer a cuddle or hug to suppress a child's anger, they will have outbursts to get attention and cuddles - not a good idea!

Once anger is let out, kids feel calmer and a cuddle can be linked to times of good Communication, comfort and courage for the future.

---

www.brahmakumaris.org for understanding anger triggers.

Communicating and Behaviour

Traffic lights of behaviours

It may help your kid to learn the **traffic lights of behaviours:**

Green is feeling good and being kind, and communicating with words.

Yellow is feeling angry, sad or scared, as everyone does and expressing it appropriately with words rather than behaviours.

Swearing profusely, glaring and threatening is still Yellow but it is best to support a child before they get to this level of distress, as it can go to Red in a split second.

Red is usually beyond words. Red is hitting, kicking, biting, smashing someone else's things or trashing a room and causing damage. It is extreme angry behaviour that hurts someone else or their belongings. It is unacceptable and illegal. It is crucial to watch for triggers and deal with the underlying fear and distress.

Small children, about 2-4 years old, often flash into angry Red. If this continues as they grow older, it is usually due to a retained Moro fight or flight reflex. It is often neurological and a bit like epilepsy or the other health issues in the way it's outside a child's control. Seek effective support and strategies as soon as possible or it can become a lifetime habit. Children in 'Red' will always be experiencing fear or extreme heartache but there are safe and natural ways to solve Red outbursts.

---

bob@accesspotential.net To overcome a retained Moro reflex.

See Bob's questionnaire at **www.felicityevans.co.uk**

www.naet-europe.com

www.cease-therapy.com

www.autismangels.co.uk.

Communicating and Behaviour

Enjoy the Green times

Enjoy the Green times of good communication and easy co-operation, fun and happy experiences with your kid and tell them about your pleasure.

Always acknowledge children with positive words when they are able to self-regulate back in appropriate ways from distressed Yellow to being Green and OK.

Kids can learn to fully express their feelings and manage them without having to take them out on others.

It is very important for the adults around them to role-model this, so children can learn this easily and for it to be their norm.

This then builds a reserve of inner resilience that can carry on into adult life.

www.felicityevans.co.uk The Heartache to Happiness Box Activity here can help many kids express their heartache with words rather than behaviours, and this lessens any distress.

www.naturaldads.com For supporting Green times, also nice for mums.

Communicating and Behaviour

Say what you want your kid to do

Say what you want your kid to do rather than giving them a 'Don't' and telling them what you don't want them to do.

If you say 'Don't tease your friend', they'll now have a picture of teasing in their mind and for some kids this becomes a compulsion. They might even repeat this over and over again.

If you suggest water and bubbles to play with, making a camp, relaxing with a DVD, going out to play a sport, then this will be the picture in their mind and they will usually stop teasing their friend.

Then they are more likely to divert to purposeful play and happy activity.

Explaining exactly what you want from your child, at certain times and in certain situations, is a kind thing to do.

This is one of the most important types of communication to have with your child.

It helps your kid feel secure and happy.

Communicating and Behaviour

Sorry, please and thank you

Most parents would like their kids to be kind and caring, polite and thoughtful.

'Sorry, please and thank you' may seem an important part of the above virtues.

But many kids nowadays are using these terms in an automatic way without any feeling. If asked to say 'Sorry', some can call it out in a derogatory way. 'Please' can even be used in a nagging way. 'Thank you' might always need a reminder.

Then these virtues become a sour response rather than a heartfelt expression.

'Sorry' doesn't make up for a wrongdoing, especially if it is something like hurting another kid. You can solve the heartache that might be leading to anger in your kid and explain the qualities and virtues that work better in life. It's more productive to enable your kid to get life right in the first place, rather than rely on 'Sorry' as a way out of getting it wrong. To solve the problem of another parent wanting your child to say sorry, you can apologise for them, adding that you will discuss it with your child later.

Forced platitudes do not necessarily create polite kids in the long run.

If your kid often hears 'please', they will most likely use it of their own accord.

It is rewarding to hear a genuine 'Thank you' occasionally, rather than one a child has been asked to say.

If young children are role-modelled 'Sorry, Please and Thank you' naturally and warmheartedly, they will copy this pattern and be kind and caring, polite and thoughtful.

The best type of words for Communicating

Kids like to know outcomes

Kids like to know outcomes, like the baby expecting an 'Ow!' after they pull your hair. You can teach a baby to, say, tap you on the chin for a 'whoooo' or similar. Then that becomes more familiar and just as much fun as the 'Ow!'

You can influence what your child is doing to get your attention. Show you are aware of what they are being and doing and regularly appreciate and acknowledge this. Then they don't have to do something undesirable or negative to get attention. If they are doing the opposite of what you want, this is the moment to switch from control to connection.

Connection is using kind words, encouragement and most of all a sense of enjoyment and fun. This brings your kid back to you, to wanting to be at one with you rather than being at odds with you.

Likewise if you show appreciation and have a sense of fun when your kid is being and doing what is best for you and great for them, this becomes the dominant habit.

Connect with children deeply with words, actions and feelings when they are doing what you want, as all kids want to feel connected to the person they are with.

The best type of words for Communicating

Disapproval

All kids suffer when they experience **disapproval**. It destroys self-worth or stops kids from developing worth in the first place.

Disapproval prevents a kid from building the wisdom that leads to making wise choices.

Disapproval can damage some kids for a very long while, even a lifetime.

Disapproval doesn't encourage a kid to do what you want or to get life right.

For example, be aware that swearing and words that you would prefer your child not to use at home may be part of their life in the playground, online or elsewhere. If you

discuss it in a matter of fact, kind way, then friction is avoided. Vehement disapproval can feel worse than swear words to a kid. Explain where and when swearing is appropriate, rather than just saying they can't.

Saying and drawing attention to what you don't want often confuses a kid and they may have no idea of what you actually want.

This doesn't mean that you have to put up with negative behaviours, rudeness or unkindness. As a mum or dad, it's your responsibility to enable your kid to manage and enjoy life.

Then life gets so much easier for you both.

See Disapproval article on: **www.felicityevans.co.uk**

The best type of words for Communicating

Let's put our heads together

'**Let's put our heads together**' is a phrase that can work really well with children. It can become a familiar practice, making it easier be proactive with kids when they have a problem - as opposed to them getting frustrated or distressed. Then there is usually more time for play, fun and joy!

'Let's put our heads together' works to solve practical problems like how to get the TV working again or emotional ones like a dread of phone bullying. You can adapt it to a phrase of your own - it's the sentiment that's important.

Suggesting 'Let's put our heads together' allows you to be totally present with your kid on equal footing: listening, understanding and responding. It's using connection rather than control, letting them know (and reminding you!) that how they are feeling is just as important as the tasks of the day. Remember that 'heads together' can be for creating fun times as well as solving problems.

Helping kids to expect a positive outcome that they have had a part in creating is really beneficial for them, leading to more powerful feelings of confidence and self worth, wellbeing and inner resilience.

When children feel that they are being listened to, they become good listeners. They will more likely hear and understand what you mean when you make a request. This can lead to joint discussions rather than you always needing your kid to do as you say, or for them to be getting their own way. Being heard encourages children to express themselves with words, rather than resort to negative behaviours to get attention.

Whenever anyone expresses themselves from the heart, it encourages others to do the same. It just feels real and genuine. Kids are really good with deeply heartfelt words - they come naturally to them.

Sometimes their words are almost too powerful for parents to hear. If your kid says something that is puzzling, hurtful or worrying, have courage and talk about this in your conversations with others. It is a gift for people to listen to you, as well as you having an opportunity to speak from your heart. And it usually turns out to be very helpful for the other person! Don't forget to chat about the joys of your kid as well!

With the concept of 'Let's put our heads together', a wonderful balance of communication emerges like the balance of a seesaw: listening encouraging good expression and expression encouraging good listening.

www.**headstogether**.org.uk 'Attitudes to mental health are at a tipping point,' The Duke and Duchess of Cambridge & Prince Harry.

The best type of words for Communicating

Positive commentary and acknowledgement

Positive commentary and acknowledgement create a really good connection with your kid, especially if it focuses on how they are being rather than what they are achieving. This really builds security as it confirms when they are getting life right.

'I can see you really enjoyed your lunch.'

'Thanks for clearing away your plate. That was helpful.'

'It is a pleasure to see you drawing happily. You concentrate so well.'

Instead of asking questions or making too many demands, give young kids emotional feedback on what is going on for them.

'You have brilliant concentration with your model' feels better to children than 'What are you making?'

'You are looking a bit sad. I am ready to listen if you want to tell me anything, now or in a little while' works better than 'What's the matter?'

'I'm really proud of how you are helping Granny feel better. You are very kind. We are all sad about Grandpa being ill but we can support one another.' This is fully being in the reality of a situation, yet seeing light at the end of the tunnel and encouraging hope and resilience.

Questions are demands and best avoided unless necessary.

Some kids struggle so much with survival that they can't take any demands. This is called Pathological Demand Avoidance and is becoming more usual with this generation of kids. All the strategies here greatly help to lessen PDA. Harry Thompson writes about PDA in his autobiography, *When I am in sensory overload, I lose my moral code.*

Communicating to Build Security

Self-regulate back to OK

Make sure your child has as many happy, relaxed and joyous times as possible. If there is any family stress, sadness or fear, the happy times need to be timetabled into your kid's life, with help from others when necessary so they have this as a norm to return to.

School can be asked to provide extra support for your kid during distressing or challenging times. At home, watch for what helps your kid relax, be absorbed and have fun.

If they become agitated for any reason, aim to move them back to the activity that helps them feel better. This can be technology but stay involved with what they are watching and vary it with outdoor activities that they enjoy. Some kids don't self-regulate well outdoors because of temperature changes or with it being more open. If they are on their own or with another child without an adult supporting them, they may feel out of their safety zone.

For others being outside can be one of the best ways for a kid to **self-regulate back to OK**: playing in the garden for little ones; walks, maybe with bikes and scooters for older ones. Teenagers and adults also benefit from outdoor time.

You can provide these supportive activities like a 'sandwich', before and after a stress.

'We'll have a special breakfast tomorrow, maybe pancakes. Then we have your visit to the dentist. Then we can go and play in the park.'

The 'sandwich' way of communicating works well in many situations throughout life: focusing on the positive, dealing with the negative, then back to a positive.

Try the Heartache to Happiness Box and the Feeling Better Plan at **www.felicityevans.co.uk**

Communicating to Build Security

Loving agreement of safe boundaries

If you start an outing screaming 'Don't you dare run off like that' it's stressful for you and your child. It can escalate into constant telling off. So change track. Before you set off remind them that the first part of the road is busy and boring. You and your kid can think about how to make it more interesting. Explain that as soon as they get to the park they can run as fast and as far as they like, so long as they can see you (or whatever feels appropriate for their age). This is setting a **loving agreement of safe boundaries**. It can take expertise, energy and time! But in the end it is less tiring than the 'Come here at once' or 'Don't do that'.

If you lose focus on what you have discussed and let them run off earlier, your kid will feel you aren't paying attention to them and this can make them feel insecure, even unsafe. In the long-term their behaviour may deteriorate to get your attention back.

Kids want you to be aware of what they are doing, feeling, playing and even thinking. So they may do things to get you to look at them, like sitting on upstairs window sills with their legs dangling out, climbing on roofs, hitting others.

Many are experiencing similar situations with their children nowadays. The more we talk about what the kids are doing and saying, the more we realise that they are similar in lots of ways and many parents are experiencing similar stresses.

Use the communication strategies in this book, discuss them with other mums and dads. Talk about what's working well or what's still stressful.

Other parents or family members may not talk to their children in ways that you use already or that are suggested in this book. Stick to what feels right for you in the face of criticism. If others affect your children in an adverse way, discuss it with your child to support them. Then see if you can reach a solution with the other person.

If the suggestions here can be a familiar and recognisable approach amongst the people around you, then life becomes easier for everyone.

www.felicityevans.co.uk

www.aspergerexperts.com offers great help with meltdowns!

Communicating to Build Security

In the moment

Most kids are completely **in the moment.**

Your kid may agree to do something in a little while or a few days later but then not carry this through. They may appear completely willing at the time, so it is exhausting and frustrating when they cannot do what has been agreed.

This isn't being naughty or thoughtless. To a child, agreeing to do something is completely different to actually doing it! They want to please you and the 'agreeing' feels kindest and best for you. They cannot think ahead to what they are meant to be carrying out or stopping. Most haven't the awareness that saying one thing, then doing another, doesn't work for you!

If you offer a second helping of food, they may say 'Yes please,' but not eat it. They say what they think you would like to hear.

If timing is important, try and keep to discussing then immediately carrying through.

Some kids can't think ahead. If you ask them if they want to see a film later in the week, they genuinely may not know if they want to go.

Sometimes not doing something, or not being able to stop something, can be linked to certain types of anxiety. Suddenly they may have an inner panic that you can't see. This can range from an uneasy feeling to a full-blown fear. At other times the panic can emerge as tears or rage. Return to what you know they can manage and build up things like outings in small steps. It's hard for a kid when they want to do something but fear stops them. Reduce the anxiety with the suggestions in this book.

Children take time to adapt to the subtleties of communication. Rather than be annoyed, we can explain and encourage so everyone feels satisfied, heard and understood.

Communicating to Build Security

Asking your kid if they want to help

Asking your kid if they want to help works better than asking them to help.

If they want to help, thank them and explain what needs to be done.

Usually a kid will want to help occasionally.

If it is always a no, use positive action/positive consequence.

Sometimes this can be realistic for some older kids: 'I have £10 to spend. Shall I pay Lizzie to tidy your room or would you like to do it? Then we can use that money to go bowling.'

Communicating to Build Security

Struggle with communication

Kids who **struggle with communication** often find learning more difficult in school and life. Some may struggle with reading as it is tricky for them to understand the content. Others may not be able to transform their creativity, knowledge, information or thoughts into essays.

Dyslexia is linked to vision (how the brain sees) but it can also delay communication. Vision can be helped by exercises, as in *Magic Eyes* by Leo Angart or the programmes provided by behavioural optometrists. As vision improves, children find it easier to read, improving their understanding and communication. Then reading is more pleasurable!

Some kids with autism may have semantic pragmatic difficulties. These can be addressed with special programmes for

communication, making life easier for them and the whole family.

Communication is essential to make positive connections with others. Without close connections, kids are more likely to be anxious and depressed. Good communication, empathy and inference are needed to study most subjects. Solve difficulties so your child can communicate easily and study what they want.

In schools that have communication as a priority, kids tend to do extra well in their studies and wellbeing.

When you can discover the root causes and work with them, this can bring about amazing results. Working on the inner health of a child and providing the right environment gives children their best chances to communicate well.

Educating Ruby by Bill Lucas and Guy Claxton.

www.charactereducation.co A headteacher's advice on developing good character.

www.jubileecentre.ac.uk/1635/character-education Character curriculum in schools.

www.fixers.org.uk Autism programme.

Communicating to Build Security

Effective communication

Effective communication is a great gift to give a kid.

Each word that you say to your kid is wiring their brain up for their future. How they speak to you is practising for their future.

Communication builds character, self-worth and inner resilience.

Communication is the key to learning, in life and in school.

Communication enhances play, creativity and leisure.

Communication leads to healthy, happy relationships.

Communication is crucial for friendship and to be kind and caring.

Communication leads to purposeful work.

Communication leads to a feeling of connection and happiness.

Resolving Part 1

*'I enjoyed that journey.
Thanks for making it fun'.*

Resolving

Introduction

The Resolving Step may seem the most challenging for some mums and dads but for most kids this Step can be important and liberating!

Children from tots to teens want to be really true to themselves and to reach their full potential in ways that are important for them. They want the freedom to develop new skills, which usually turn out to be important for life today. Kids want change, to be innovative and to be loving, caring and kind - so they like the 6 Steps, even Resolving! For some children this section could be seen as a prevention of future difficulties and this can be a motivation for parents too.

Many refuse to repeat family patterns and there is an increase in the number of children showing varied, marked differences early in life: by not speaking; by withdrawing from the demands of everyday life (passively or violently); with challenging behaviours; school refusal; patterns from autism and anorexia; addictions to alcohol and drugs. Some may be exposing their deep heartache and want to swing the pendulum back from their inner struggles to an authentic, natural way of being. These patterns used to emerge in older teenagers, then younger teenagers and now primary aged children or even toddlers! It used to be a few kids but now it's many. Some will really challenge their parents' familiar ways. This may seem annoying, a problem or a huge challenge but it's the children's attempt to match who they are to the effective lifestyles of today.

So as a parent you are not alone. But because of how the health and education systems work at the moment, it seems like you have to manage on your own and you may even be seen as being in the wrong. You are not. Trust your parental instinct first and go with that.

Some of these pages hold the exhaustion, frustration and stress of real mums and dads and the fear, anguish and heartache of children. These pages are not here to cause pain or guilt but to bring hope and healing.

Seek support and use the ideas in this book to come to a point of harmony between you and your kid and, whenever possible, between you and the health or education authorities until you get all the support you need.

Life may seem like an endless battle with your kid and even more so with the authorities. But the children who have gone before have been pioneering new ways of life ready for your child, so you are not alone.

We are looking for win/win. This is when both of you feel heard, understood and happy.

If this section becomes familiar and part of everyday focus, we can carefully resolve what is making life tricky for our kids and life can become so much easier, even wonderful!

Resolving Part 1 Contents

Resolving and Change

Need their world to change

What may seem relatively normal, acceptable and appropriate to some parents may be overwhelming and frightening to their kids. If your kid is completely well and happy and managing and enjoying life, they are in 'happiness'. If they are showing negative behaviours by being withdrawn or feeling unwell, they may be overloaded and overwhelmed - in 'heartache'.

They **need their world to change**, maybe a little, maybe dramatically. This can happen by using the suggestions, ideas and strategies in this book. Little steps towards change can build up into amazing breakthroughs with your child.

Some may also need a spectrum of support for their emotional, physical and mental health and general wellbeing. Very often natural therapies can bring about changes and enrich life for everyone in the family.

The Caveman Principles: Get rid of everyday stress and enjoy mammoth success! by Carl Rosier -Jones

Carl offers a great way to look at change on his website: **www.carlrosierjones.com**

Resolving and Change

Never, ever blame your kid for negative traits

Often a first step towards change is to check that you **never, ever blame your kid for negative traits** that they have inherited from their other parent, or other family members.

Instead use all your energy to enable them to develop all their positive traits and move towards improvements and solutions for what is stressful.

It works really well to say, 'We don't like it if X doesn't turn up but we can still love them.' Children may still have a strong bond and loyalty to those who stress them. It is helpful to distinguish the differences between who people are and what they do or don't do, which could be dire for a child.

Avoid drawing attention to inherited patterns like anger that you want to lessen in your kid. Instead build kindness and caring. Give support for anger to be expressed in safe and appropriate ways.

Especially avoid comments like 'Y was always hopeless at reading,

so I expect that's why you can't read.' This can give a kid a limiting belief for a lifetime. Instead find ways for your child to learn to read a small step at a time, giving loads of encouragement and support. Your kid can learn to read with the knowledge and understanding we have nowadays. Looking at vision (how their brain sees) is a useful first step.

The good things can be your focus, especially if your kid expresses concern about any inherited aspect of their life such as anger. Children nowadays can have very deep feelings and a knowing about inherited tendencies. They can't ignore them and it is very important for them to become confident about their inheritance and who they are.

Children can be competently supported with cultural and religious differences and if they have two nationalities.

Differences can be celebrated and your kid can build inner peace, security, a love of self and kindness towards all others.

Resolving and Change

The Big Feeling

It's really helpful for children to be able to name **The Big Feeling** when they have a negative one that pervades their day. This can be something that originates from an emotion that they feel or that comes as a result of what another person is saying or doing.

Children have strong feelings of their own and can gradually learn to not feel too overwhelmed by the intensity. Then it's easier to express all feelings appropriately. It's helpful for kids if you encourage them to talk about their Big Feeling: having to read aloud in class; the loss of a pet; being teased or bullied. This is a time when your child needs your full attention and support - they need to feel fully heard and understood. Kids want you to be very proactive and help them manage and process this feeling. If they say they have a Big Feeling about not being able to have an ice cream, think about low blood sugar and any underlying stress of the moment. Ice creams aren't a reason for The Big Feeling!

When a child has a Big Feeling from what another person is saying or doing, they want this resolved, right now. Some kids (and adults) live in situations where what someone else is doing gives them the feeling 'You are affecting me to such a degree that it is really difficult for me to feel OK now or in the future'. The Big Feeling pervades their day. Adults have more awareness of situations changing and their ability to recover from strong feelings, but children don't have this inner reserve.

We can't change other people, only ourselves, but we do need to create a culture where everyone builds an awareness of how their actions or words affect others. Excessive anger or control are overt and will always give a child a Big Feeling but then so do the less overt yet often ongoing patterns of anxiety, depression and grief.

We can build a culture where anger, control, anxiety, depression and grief receive understanding, compassion and support from others. Naming these emotions isn't being weak or feeling a victim - it's coming into natural positive power, to create solutions and work towards feeling better. If you are on the receiving end of another's unacceptable behaviour, you can come to an agreement as to when specific support is needed in order to find solutions. If we look at root causes, there are highly effective ways for anyone to deal with all these issues, as described in this book and the listed resources.

If we help children learn about their Big Feelings then they can let go of the negative ones and establish a Big Feeling of kindness, joy, fun, laughter and love.

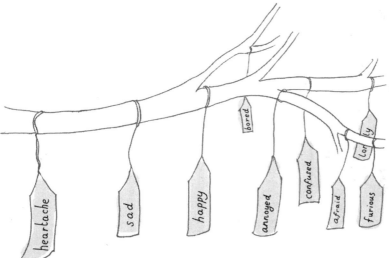

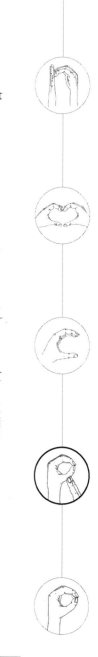

The Five Side Effects of Kindness by Dr David Hamilton.

Resolving and Change

Sense tension

Kids nowadays are usually very intuitive, knowing and clever. This has absolutely nothing to do with academic achievement.

They can **sense tension** from others towards themselves or between two people, especially with family members.

This can be minor tension like getting lost in the car, when one person suggests one way and someone else another.

Children also immediately sense adults' stress over something like losing a job or redundancy. If parents are going to divorce or if there is major illness in the family, they feel the build-up of tension.

We can't always protect our kids from life's dramas and stresses but we can care for them, if we seek our own support first.

---

www.michaeljames.be It doesn't matter how you are feeling, you can always feel better. Michael offers practical and groundbreaking ideas for when you feel low or uninspired to enjoying life, feeling good and creating the life you want.

www.actionforhappiness.org This website helps people take action for a happier and more caring world. It also runs local support groups.

Resolving Anger

Getting to the end of your tether

Kids will survive and flourish when adults are honest about anger and easily and naturally come back to being kind and caring. Be real not fake, as children can see through this straightaway.

If you find yourself **getting to the end of your tether** too often with your child, build yourself more slack! This can be incredibly hard. Others may not understand that you need recharge time. We are not used to looking after ourselves and may feel guilty asking for help or spending money on childcare. You may have a child who doesn't want you to leave them, ever. Go back to read about anxiety and lessen it by looking at Freeze, Flight and Fright. Use the strategy of tiny steps. Start with leaving them for two minutes early in the day before they are tired. Build it up over time until they are happy to be left with others, even at bedtime.

Find a way to have some more recharge time before you get too tired, frustrated or annoyed. Not so long ago most parents had the extended family nearby and this gave not only parents a break but also the children had another place to go when they needed a change.

Sometimes we hang onto things more when we are tired. Ask yourself 'How important is this?' Look after your own wellbeing and check yourself before reprimanding your child.

If you do get angry with your kid, give them space to recover. Avoid a placatory 'sorry' as this makes a child feel worse. Reflect on the situation and aim to get back to normal everyday life. Then, when you feel calm, apologise from your heart and show your deepest love and affection. This role-models that love and affection are part of normal, calm life.

Resolving Anger

Excessive anger

Anger becomes easier to manage when you consider both your feelings on the inside and the external triggers. **Excessive anger** is when you feel angry all the time or when you have outbursts that shock or terrify others. Anger can stem from many sources: a family tendency of shouting vehemently in order to be heard; allergies or what was eaten for breakfast; low blood sugar; an extra Y chromosome; differing brain patterns; the surfacing of very painful memories, abuse or trauma; feeling bullied in school, home or elsewhere; poor self-worth and a lack of identity; a need for revenge or control to survive; exhaustion and stress.

First acknowledge any anger you have then seek all the support you need to disperse your anger so your kid or others are not on the receiving end of it. People who have these neurological patterns need everyone's support, not to be seen as terrible people. If we remove the stigma of anger and give it support like grief, these patterns can be changed in our brains, bringing back the freedom to be kind, caring, calm and positive.

Practice stopping your fight, flight or freeze reflex from ruling your day.

If needed, there is effective support and good complementary medicine, as well as the GP to help you do this.

We can help children learn that our anger wells up inside us and we are responsible for it, even if there is an external trigger.

Role-model: 'I'm feeling too angry. I'll go to my room give myself space.' Then return to being loving and supportive as soon as possible.

Anger management:

www.brahmakumaris.org

www.michaeljames.be

www.bemindful.co.uk

www.naet-europe.com

The Caveman Principles by Carl Rosier-Jones.

www.naturaldads.com It's also nice for mums to read.

Resolving Anger

All kids are distressed by all anger

Occasionally we need to use loud, firm voices to quickly get our kid's attention: 'Please stop before the road,' or 'Please come here,' if they are about to hurt or take something from another kid. But anger never controls or improves a situation. All children need help in understanding the difference between what we are doing to keep them safe and happy, from when we are expressing undeserved anger, inappropriate intervention or unhealthy control. Observe how your kid is reacting to what you are saying.

All kids are distressed by all anger - even their own. If the fear of a loved one's anger pervades their whole day, they may express anxiety and hyper-vigilance with negative behaviours. Being angry with a child doesn't improve their behaviour. They may see spilling their drink as similar to poking a friend in the eye with a stick and use 'I didn't mean to do

it'. Many don't tell the truth to avoid parents' anger, as they can't handle it.

If kids get their homework wrong, anger never enables them to learn better. It usually blocks learning, often long term. Kind support works scientifically better for brains and has many benefits for those being kind!

Use discussion to prepare a child for something: 'How are we going to sort out you turning your iPad off and getting your shoes on, so I can get to the dentist on time?' Reach an agreement. Then if your child doesn't manage this, you can say it feels stressful and the stress is making you angry. It is better to explain how you experience the situation rather than blame them, as this usually delays getting out.

Increasing kindness, happiness and joy helps children co-operate more and manage getting out on time easily.

www.actionforhappiness.org

The Five Side Effects of Kindness by Dr David Hamilton.

Resolving Anger

Being on the receiving end of powerful anger

When you are angry, your child may appear nonchalant - in fact often the more nonchalant they are the more fear they may be feeling. So without judging yourself or them, seek whatever strategies you need for your anger to subside. Anger can be like hay fever, triggered by the combination of what is inside you and what is around you.

When the internet or TV has made suggestions about how to control a child and your kid doesn't take to this, don't get frustrated with them. Likewise don't blame yourself for not getting the strategy to work. All kids are unique and the pioneer type kids need innovative ideas. They will respond to what works for them so try different ways to build co-operation.

Nowadays there is easy access to the support needed for managing possibly inherited or ingrained patterns, like anger.

Feeling subservient, abused or **being on the receiving end of powerful anger** can neurologically prevent a kid from being able to develop, mature or function.

Lessening your anger is an important gift for you to give your kid or the anger will perpetuate into the next generation, often at an enhanced level. Sometimes we, or our kids, have to get to a massive overload of anger before we think about taking steps towards wellbeing. But the sooner the courage is there to take these steps, the quicker the stress is overcome, and the joyful times can return.

All the natural therapies, and support groups and coaches listed in this book can help with lessening anger.

www.brahmakumaris.org

Childhood Disrupted: How Your Biography Becomes Your Biology, and How You Can Heal by Donna Jackson Nakazawa.

Resolving Anger

Manage feelings more easily

Avoid making your kid responsible for how you are feeling: 'You are making me tired/angry/frustrated/annoyed/worried/ depressed/ despairing/feel ill/giving me a headache,' or even 'If you do this I won't be tired then we can go out to play.'

Instead role model that you will take the responsibility for how you are feeling.

Then children can learn how to **manage feelings more easily** and learn eventually that, if they are not feeling OK, there are steps that they can take to help themselves feel better - self-regulating.

If they see being distressed as always someone else's fault, it can lead to constant blaming and scapegoating and this delays their ability to resolve issues and aim for win/win situations, where both sides are happy with the outcome.

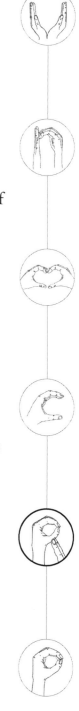

Resolving Anger

Confused messages about anger and love

Many children don't know how to ask nicely for attention and get **confused messages about anger and love**.

An example of this is a parent coming in from work and having chores to do, yet naturally the child wants attention. The parent may calmly be getting a meal but the child pesters more and more until the parent loses patience and shouts at them. The kid's face crumples and tears come into their eyes. The parent stops what they are doing and bends down to cuddle the child. This is not an unusual situation but if it continues long-term, the child will escalate beyond pestering and start to be belligerent. This can become a pattern of the child increasing negative behaviours to get to the attention, the hug and the love. Some children are deliberately belligerent to get to the cuddle.

Some parents may use a hug or cuddle to soothe away a child's rage. But it's better to show love first before your kid gets angry. Give them a few minutes before the chores and chat to them about what you are doing. Then kids don't need to use anger or belligerence to get your love and attention.

Another scenario may be a mum or dad coming home from work after an extremely stressful day. They are still feeling uptight, possibly very angry. The child drops their coat on the floor, walks in with dirty shoes, and mum or dad explode. The child runs to hide in their room because they feel that they have caused their parent's anger. They didn't. The coat and the shoes provided an outlet for the parent's temper but the cause was from work. Once the exasperation is out, the parent can sense the child's distress and run up to comfort them.

If you are highly stressed from work or other situations, explain to your child that you are, without worrying them. Say you need a moment to collect yourself and then give them loving attention. It can be soothing and take your mind off the coat and shoes. That can be dealt with later. Choose the nice times first.

Resolving Anger

Kind and caring

We want our kids to be **kind and caring**. If they are behaving in an aggressive way towards another child, we tell them off, even if the other child has initiated the problem. But this gives them mixed messages: 'I am being angry with you, but you mustn't be angry.' Instead encourage kids to express their anger and sort things out without aggression.

Some children kick or hit as hard as they can, especially siblings or parents. This is different from a token push for 'Out of my way' or 'Leave me alone'. They may quickly say 'Sorry'. Some parents then give a cuddle because they are so relieved that the physical aggression has stopped. Yet this is wiring up the brain to use aggression to get a cuddle. This gives them very confused messages and can affect them long term.

Increase the times you offer more attention. Find physical ways that don't hurt others for them to let out anger. Explore the root causes of their anger, which usually comes from some type of fear. Give comfort, reassurance and support for the distress that is causing the anger. Ensure that your child has a way to receive loving attention, without having to kick or rage.

When they are playing happily, often give attention. Offer love before they have to seek it.

Resolving Anger

Vehement firmness

Vehement firmness can break through a negative situation if used very occasionally. Use one or two firm, loud words like 'Stop', if a kid is running towards a busy road or 'Come here', if a kid is hurting another kid.

But don't just use the 'Come here' to stop the hurting. Immediately take responsibility for your own child and explain clearly if their behaviour is unacceptable. It's good if the child on the receiving end of being hurt hears that too, otherwise they may be set on retaliation. Discuss alternative ways to sort out a situation. With a small one use something along the lines of: 'I saw that you wanted to go on the slide first. It's tricky to wait. Shall I come and play with you while you are waiting on the steps?' This is a crucial learning situation. An automatic 'Sorry' isn't going to help kids make better choices in the future. With older kids, help them find the words to sort the situation with another child: 'I feel angry and left out when you always let my friend go down the slide first. I don't like always being last. Can I go first sometimes?'

Later explain to your child why you had to be vehement and use a firm 'Come here'. If you were a bit too loud for them, apologise and look to how you can prevent needing to shout in the future.

If a kid hears constant disapproval or the same type of correction for spilling a drink as hurting another kid, they don't learn the difference, or take notice, or adapt what they do.

Chat in a gentle and kind way about the behaviours that end up with negative outcomes and encourage what works well.

Resolving Anger

Let out normal feelings of anger appropriately

Young kids can let out their anger by playing 'angry lions' or 'angry robots'. They can thump a soft sofa or cushion as hard as they can, and scream as loudly as they can - show them how to do this. Older kids can have punchballs.

This gives them a way to **let out normal feelings of anger appropriately**, without dumping it on someone else.

If anger is expressed appropriately, it doesn't lead to aggression.

Enable your kid to manage their triggers: fatigue, fears, frustration, family patterns. Use purposeful words and discussions with your kid, rather than sudden, vehement outbursts or disapproval which can damage a kid for years.

Suppressed or disapproved of anger often does lead to unwanted behaviours. It is never OK for a kid to bully or hurt someone else to get rid of their anger, and the earlier they can learn about this the easier life will be for them, long-term.

www.felicityevans.co.uk See the PDA Disapproval article on my website.

Resolving and Structure

Think about No

Think about No. For many kids, when you say No, it feels like you don't love them. Children don't have a concept of 'it is for your own good'! This takes a lot of understanding and maturation. And they don't understand why they can't always have the new toy they fancy. Explanations need to feel right, as they won't see the logic - like you need to buy food not the toy. Discussions need regular practice. Delayed gratification takes time to learn and manage, and only happens for real once there is a strong sense of wellbeing and inner strength.

If you use Yes or No without thinking, then keep changing your mind, your kid may become a nagger, constantly pestering you. In this case changing your mind makes them feel insecure. An example of this might be your child asking before school if someone can come to play at teatime. If you initially say yes but change your mind at the end of the day because you've made other plans, you may get a tantrum.

Children don't like 'maybe', but sometime it's fairer than yes or no.

Aim to avoid No most of the time and replace it with nurturing words, adapted to the age of your kid.

Kids often run out of school asking if a friend can come round to play. If you know this isn't going to be possible in advance, remind them: 'Remember Gran is coming round for tea and she hasn't been very well. She will want to have a quiet time. So we will see if one of your friends can come round tomorrow.' This avoids the No at the end of the day.

If kids are helped to cope as often as possible, then they have the inner resources to cope when there has to be a 'not now', 'later' or 'I don't think that's going to be possible'.

Look to the reason *why* children are asking for things and help them manage this. Then life is easier for everyone.

Resolving and Structure

Avoid smacking

Some may say that a quick slap on the leg can stop a child misbehaving - but it doesn't in the long term.

When kids misbehave, it's their way of saying 'I can't manage this situation'. If the intervention is supportive rather than punishing, they start to manage and their behaviour improves. They feel better.

We want children to learn to use words, not behaviours. And they will if those around them model this. **Avoiding smacking** will improve a child's behaviour.

If smacking has been a family pattern for a long time and you want this to stop, set aside the time to help the kids express their heartache, before they are letting it out with negative behaviours for which you may have given them a smack. Younger kids you can use the 'Heartache to Happiness box' technique, where emptying their jewels or marbles from the box indicates they are feeling heartache. Then you find ways for them to feel better, to put their jewels or marbles back. For older ones, chose an activity you both enjoy and once they are feeling relaxed, you can encourage them to chat to you about their feelings and what's going on for them.

Some kids find it difficult to discuss and negotiate. They need help with this as young as possible, as in Step 4 Communicating, so they build the necessary tools for life and inner resilience.

Connecting with children and meeting their need for love and attention, rather than trying harder and harder to control them, will always improve co-operation and lead to easier happier lives for everyone.

No-Drama Discipline by Daniel Siegel and Tina Payne Bryson.

Resolving and Structure

Punishment

Punishment usually increases anxiety and negative behaviours and destroys self-worth.

What kids are doing is either coming from heartache or happiness.

If a child has an illness, you give them nurture and support. They need the same for their feelings and behaviours.

Punishing a child is saying they have no worth at that moment. They may not be able to override that feeling.

Then as the negative feelings increase, the negative behaviours will increase.

Use simple structure and mutually agreed boundaries for your kid to feel safe and to make the best choices.

Resolving with Choice

Building wellbeing

Some parents are so exhausted and stressed that they come to a stop. They ask even small children to do all the household chores, including cleaning and preparing a meal. This is not the same as when a child is a formal carer for a parent.

Ideally you will be able to role-model to your child that chores are OK and they will naturally help, especially with tasks that are related to their life.

The aim of this book is to find life easier with the kids - to get out of the vicious circle of exhausting child and exhausted parent, stressing child and stressed parent.

This is the time to resolve exhaustion and stress. Understand yourself, nurture yourself, love yourself, communicate your needs and find time for your play.

Most people nowadays are in the third generation of increasing stress and exhaustion, leading to poor health. So let's think about **building wellbeing**. I find 'wellbeing' a boring word but it indicates vitality, enthusiasm, fun and joy. Start with the body - eat nutritious foods that give you energy and do activities that recharge you. Find others who want to focus on happiness. Share positive thoughts and be emotionally supportive. Take time to have fun and laugh - with kids and adults. Try 'Handing Over' - at the end of Nurturing Part 2.

Aim for the energy to do the 6 Steps in this book, to support your child so they are less exhausting and stressing, naturally becoming more rewarding and fun.

The Caveman Principles: Get rid of everyday stress and enjoy mammoth success by Carl Rosier-Jones.

www.michaeljames.be For Handing Over, website, groups and book.

www.actionofhappiness.org

www.naet.com For detox and better absorption of nutrients.

www.rodwellhypnotherapy.co.uk Fulfil your potential, release obstacles and pain.

The Coupledom Trap by Tal Araim. MOTs for couples.

Resolving with Choice

Choose how you want your kid to be

Choose how you want your kid to be with you, rather than feel a victim because of what they are doing.

Talk through their day with them in advance, check out how they are feeling and managing, give regular commentary of what they are doing well or gently enable them to come back to effective and appropriate behaviours.

At the end of the day, rather than recap their academic successes, spend time acknowledging who they are and how well they are doing. Say how much you love them.

Chat about the fun you had with them and how much you enjoy the sound of their laughter.

Talk about joy. If you've not had much time for joy because of the school run, your work and their homework, take time to be with them before they go to bed, maybe reading a book, making up stories or telling jokes.

Acknowledge how good it feels to be with them. This builds self-worth and self-identity.

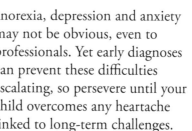

Resolving with Choice

Bigger challenges

Some kids face **bigger challenges** in life than others. This could be a bereavement, a serious illness, a major accident or differences like a hearing impairment and restricted vision. Offering these kids all the support that they deserve at these times, at home and in school, needs to be a priority and ongoing. It is crucial for their mental wellbeing now and in their future lives as adults.

When there is something obvious that can be seen or measured, assessed or diagnosed medically, children are more likely to receive understanding, compassion and support. This enhances their inner resilience.

Some challenges are not so visible like dyslexia, autism, and PDA and this may make it harder for a child and their families to get a diagnosis, let alone adequate support. In their early stages,

anorexia, depression and anxiety may not be obvious, even to professionals. Yet early diagnoses can prevent these difficulties escalating, so persevere until your child overcomes any heartache linked to long-term challenges.

Some young people feel at odds with their birth gender from quite young. Parents may need even more help with this than their kid because it is outside their experience.

All the strategies in this book work for kids to be as happy as possible when valued for themselves and whatever their circumstances.

By letting go of our fixed beliefs, children can naturally develop amazing strengths, shine from their hearts and enrich our lives - sometimes in ways beyond anything we could imagine.

www.childbereavementuk.org

www.mermaidsuk.org.uk Family support for children with gender identity issues.

www.autism.org.uk

www.dyslexiaaction.org.uk

Resolving with Choice

Focus on developing the inner resources

Avoid placating your kid, or doing anything just for a quiet life, as this can lead to tricky situations escalating and feelings of insecurity.

Instead **focus on developing the inner resources** they need to cope with everyday life, supporting their health and wellbeing at the same time.

If your child wants every toy they see in the supermarket and you buy the toy to keep them quiet, they will crave more and more because the toy is not making them happy in the long-term.

Practise looking around without buying the toy or book or game. Explain the practicalities of this. Reassure them that you love them even when you can't buy everything they want. Check how they are feeling and think about why it is that they need something to cheer them up. With younger children, have something they like to play with when you go into a shop so they are not bored. Increase fun times.

If kids always demand their own way, this can increase until things are unmanageable. Before you give in to constant demands (checking they are more than reasonable requests), explore what is going on. Demanding kids are usually brimful of stress: physical from a sensory overload and toxicity, neurological from differing brain patterns and emotional from retained reflexes constantly triggering their freeze, fight or flight response. They use their own demands, or avoid demands from others, to try to calm themselves. Use the ways in this book to lessen their physical, neurological and emotional distress.

In daily life, help your child to manage waiting and flexibility in tiny steps, say, by giving interesting things for them to do while you wash up. Then the natural and happy consequence is that you can find time for what they want to do.

Resolving Circumstances

Making travel more enjoyable for your kid

Most kids don't find travel enjoyable and some absolutely hate being restrained in a car seat or by a seat belt or having to stop in a traffic jam, even to the point of panic.

From the start, the focus can be on **making travel more enjoyable for your kid**.

It only takes a moment to put a favourite toy, book or comic in the car before you take your kid to the car. As they get older they can choose themselves. For kids who do better with novelty, you can see if there is a free bookshop in your area or collect little surprises from charity shops. When going on buses, you can have a nice distraction in your bag as well as your phone - if that's what they usually play on! If they are on your phone, be really interested in what they are doing.

Even when you have to concentrate on driving, this is still a good time to be fully present for your kid. Older kids often express themselves well in a car as there aren't so many distractions.

Younger kids in a car or bus can look out for things you suggest: a red car, a green lorry, a dog, a man in glasses with a hat on a bicycle! It doesn't take much of your focus and it can completely take away a young child's boredom.

Resolving Circumstances

You need calm and quiet to drive the car safely

If your kid is noisy or disruptive in the car, on their own or with others, stop the car in a safe place and explain that **you need calm and quiet to drive the car safely**. Wait for this before driving on.

If disruption is a common pattern, explain that you would like to take them swimming but are not sure if they can manage the journey safely. Many kids are anxious about not managing so you need to talk supportively. Put nice things in the car for experiential distractions - maybe a comic and water to drink. Talk about what you will do after swimming as some kids find it hard to manage stopping activities that they particularly love. Ideally you will enable them to manage the journey easily. If not return home and wait for a day when they can be ready to be safe in the car. Anger will not solve situations like this - just creativity and calm!

Some children need to discuss swimming or other outings for days in advance, to get used to the idea. Others need to be near the swimming pool when you ask if they want to swim, so they can go straight to the pool without it playing on their mind. Being in the car can feel very different to a child - different to what we might imagine.

If someone else's kid is disruptive, remind them about safety. Explain that if they can't manage, you may need to call their parent/carer to come and fetch them. Again this is not a threat. It is merely something you are going to calmly carry through. Most kids will understand safety and settle down.

Calm and quiet can sometimes be more to do with attitude than noise level. Many kids love singing in the car, on their own or to the radio. Also some very positive car games can be noisy, but this is different noise to agitation, arguments and disruption. Singing and fun can enhance concentration for the driver.

Resolving Circumstances

Less likely to become obsessed with their computer

Computers are a natural part of everyday life for kids nowadays.

They are extremely entertaining, informative and fun. For some, the communication linked to a computer will create a career. This can happen naturally and effortlessly.

Just check that your child isn't using the computer in place of reality, friendship and life. If these are going well, they are **less likely to become obsessed with their computer** or tablet, computer games, and social media.

Computers can frazzle some brains, cause sleep disturbance and block a kid from coming into the fullness of themselves. But they are also a source of pleasure, fun and varied information. Be interested in their screen time and make it a joint pleasure.

Avoid 'coming off the computer' battles. Provide lots of interesting activities and structure.

If children develop a wide range of interests, being on a computer or sharing with like-minded 'friends' on social media can remain a source of enjoyment.

The Loneliness Cure: Six Strategies for Finding Real Connections in Your Life by Kory Floyd, MD. For adults to role-model a balance in social media.

Resolving Part 2

'That's great climbing!'

Resolving Part 2 Contents

Active Intervention

Active Intervention includes the usual actions your child experiences with you in everyday life: meals, reading a story, stopping them from running in the road, helping with homework, saying it's bedtime.

Children don't always experience these interventions as being for their wellbeing and safety!

So it works best when you are fully focused and prepare your kid for what is about to happen, rather than give them the experience of a sudden outburst or desperate final attempt for something to happen.

Often these requests can be turned into games or fun for a small child, or pleasurable times for an older one. Like sitting with them when they start homework and lightening the task. If they have to write a poem about 'Butterflies' and they don't want to start, they may like their poem to describe being fed up with 'Butterfly' tasks.

Always appreciate and acknowledge when your kid easily and naturally co-operates with these types of requests, as you would with an adult if they were helpful.

Resolving and the Interactions: Active and Increased

Agreements and information

When you have to actively intervene to get your kid to do something that they don't want to do, or stop doing something they don't want to stop, prepare (get ready), pre-empt (think if there might be a problem and how you may best meet their needs) and pre-pave (explain confidently and clearly) to enable them to do the task in hand easily, without stress.

Very occasionally give a firm 'Stop' or 'No' when they are doing something destructive for themselves or others. Find a calm moment as soon as possible to give an explanation. Have a chat, with **agreements and information** for them to explore what would work so they know more about how to manage and cope.

Make it fun when possible and hugely increase all that they love and enjoy, so limitations aren't overwhelming.

If your kid doesn't comply with reasonable requests, they may be in overload from negative interventions.

Have a think about this and reduce negative interventions as much as possible, so requests are easier for them to carry out and life for everyone is pleasant.

No-Drama Discipline by Daniel Siegel and Tina Payne Bryson.

Increased Interaction

Increased Interaction is checking that you are helping your child to mature. This can be encouraging them to move on from the actions of little ones like sleeping in your bed to having adequate, good sleep on their own to recharge for the next day. Keep an eye on nourishment (the body and brain are made up of what goes into them) and how easily your kid manages and enjoys meals. Support friendships and interests and ensure good free 'Time to be', outdoors when possible.

It is encouraging your kid with their passion for football when yours is sailing, letting them daydream when they could be tidying their room. It is paying more attention to their feelings than getting homework done.

It's bringing your child to their true authenticity rather than whom you would like them to be. Look for their gifts and delights, sometimes hidden under marked differences in development, behaviours and feelings.

It is building self-worth and inner resilience.

Resolving and the Interactions: Missing and Subtle

Lessen Missing Interaction

It works really well to **lessen Missing Interaction**, as most kids struggle a lot with this.

Missing Interaction is not taking wellies for a walk on the beach in winter. And a towel, waterproofs, a full change of clothes and a large plastic bag! If your kid sees the sea they will want to paddle, and most kids don't mind getting wet or feel the cold as much as adults. Not preparing for this feels very upsetting to most kids and they may give you a meltdown or animosity later in the day, probably not even knowing why.

Likewise Missing Interaction can be as simple as forgetting the PE kit, giving them a packed lunch they don't like, or arriving late to collect them from school - this can happen to all of us sometimes but be mindful of the effect. Missing Interaction can be as serious as not standing up for them or not being very proactive - not solving the problem completely, if they feel bullied at school or misunderstood by the teacher.

Missing Interaction is frequently being on your phone or tablet in their company. Kids need you to be present much of the time, even if this is keeping an ear open for them in another room. Then they feel secure within agreed expectations.

When you are on a phone it feels to them that you are distant. This will cause some to feel anxiety.

When you are with your kid, one good idea may be to sometimes turn off your smartphone which can absorb a lot of your time and attention. Some use a separate, basic phone that just does texts and calls, if you need access to these. It can have the same number as your main phone. It brings you back to being present with your kid.

Lessening Missing Interaction can be as uplifting to do as it is to watch the results.

Less than your authentic self with your kid

Missing Interaction is being **less than your authentic self with your kid.** Most kids nowadays can see deep inside people, who they really are, and they may react by re-acting any stresses that you are experiencing.

If your child is getting angry or withdrawn with you, there is often an element of this. They can sense when you are not OK. This can take away their security and safety and may trigger angry or withdrawn behaviours.

The other big trigger is if they feel you are taking someone else's side, especially their other parent or a sibling. Rather take a neutral stance and listen to both sides.

Not stopping another adult or child being angry or aggressive with your kid is also experienced as Missing Interaction by children, as they may feel powerless in the situation. The same applies if they are feeling bullied or upset. As well as actual verbal or physical abuse

causing distress, be aware that some kids can be suffering huge trauma from inappropriate internet material or social media, especially as this can be unseen.

When children are highly sensitive, maybe having difficulty with making or keeping friends, sometimes not yet streetwise, a bit naïve or vulnerable, they can be taken advantage of by other distressed kids. They may be desperate to be 'one of the crowd', and be sent to 'nick sweets', or become subject to internet or actual abuse. This can end up being absolutely terrifying for them and cause major changes in behaviour, sometimes leading to problematic situations.

So missed opportunities for support, even without you realising your kid wants or needs it, can cause kids to take dramatic steps to try to regain control of their own lives. Being aware and noticing distress as soon as possible brings about the best outcomes.

Resolving and the Interactions: Missing and Subtle

Increase healing the family tree

Looking out for Missing Interaction and giving intensive and appropriate help may greatly **increase healing the family tree.**

It is focusing on what is deep inside both you and your kid, bringing healing to the aspects that aren't in harmony so you can understand one another better.

This is one of the greatest gifts we can share with our kids.

Resolving and the Interactions: Missing and Subtle

Subtle Interaction

Subtle Interaction has a large impact on your kid's life because of the heightened sensitivity of many children nowadays. Most are fully aware of what others around them are feeling on a deep level: other kids or adults, even strangers.

Subtle interaction is unseen and unheard but definitely felt.

Kids need to feel confident to climb trees. Give them enough advice and initial supervision to check their climbing ability. If you feel nervous, it helps to use some mindfulness exercises for yourself, like deep breathing. Once they are old enough and adept, you can look away and relax. Empower them with confidence and enjoy the moment as much as them.

Even if you hide emotions, children often pick up on how you are feeling about the bill that needs to be paid, illness, divorce, redundancy, bereavement, a row with a relative or neighbour - anything that gives rise to anger, worry or grief in you.

Kids *feel* that these moments will go on forever but they also want to *know* that this can be transient. We all have worries sometimes but your child needs to observe you passing through feelings appropriately and as quickly as possible.

They will notice how much resilience you have and when you feel OK. You can aim to be as relaxed and happy as possible and they will really appreciate what you role-model to them.

Mindfulness for Dummies by Shamash Alidina.

www.bemindful.co.uk

www.actionforhappiness.org

www.sam-app.org.uk To understand and manage anxiety.

Resolving and the Interactions: Missing and Subtle

Make our mental wellbeing everyday conversation

Life can be very challenging nowadays but adults have a choice about their wellbeing. Many are hesitant to seek and embrace change despite knowing it would be better for everyone. In this case, people are usually stuck in their stress through the fight, flight or freeze responses of the brain stem, rather than processing feelings through the creativity of the frontal cortex. As the brain has neuroplasticity, it is possible to establish different brain pathways and thereby a different lifestyle.

Once there is an acceptance that life is currently painful for oneself or others, support and choices can be more readily available. Let's make it much easier for everyone to talk about these circumstances, to open up to a friend or coach, about any aspect of our thoughts, feelings and emotions.

Take courage from those in the public limelight who are so honest about their mental health nowadays and let's **make our mental wellbeing everyday conversation**, without any stigma.

If you have a broken leg, putting on a plaster cast to help it recover is not seen as weakness - it's sensible and normal. Looking after our mental wellbeing affects far more people than broken legs - 1 person in 4 isn't in a plaster or limping. But 1 person in 4 does need to take special care of their mental health.

We can all keep a check on our own mental health. Sometimes we may need support and sometimes we can be there for others.

Let's make this really easy for all of us, to receive and to give. When you know someone who needs support, let go of all judgement. Offer confidence, kindness and loving attention - just as you would help a neighbour with a broken leg.

We can profoundly care for our children's mental wellbeing from birth, to build their inner resilience for whatever life presents to them.

www.felicityevans.co.uk See Bob Allen's questionnaire on my website to enable the brain to better process stress through the frontal cortex rather than the brain stem.

www.headstogether.org.uk 'Attitudes to mental health are at a tipping point,' The Duke and Duchess of Cambridge & Prince Harry.

www.museumofhappiness.org Shamash Alidina, the museum's co-founder, says 'Happiness is a skill that can be learnt.'

www.michaeljames.be Emerging journeys.

The Five Side Effects of Kindness by Dr David Hamilton, the scientific evidence to feel better, be happier, live longer.

www.drdansiegel.com/blog/2015/01/22/brain-insights-and-well-being-3/

Resolving and the Interactions: Missing and Subtle

Old expectations

Be especially careful with one type of Subtle Interaction - **old expectations**.

The old expectation may be wanting your kid to do a little bit better than you did. Partly this is natural from a parent, as they love their child. But it can be negative. For example if you want your child to do better in their studies than you did, this is saying very profoundly to your child: 'I am not very worthy and I want you to be more worthy than me.' It takes away confidence rather than encouraging self-worth. A kid doesn't want to sense lack of worth in a parent. They just want to love you.

Linking self-worth to focusing on fame and fortune never works. It is focusing on the outside world which can cause heartache, rather than the inner self which can blossom into self-worth, success and happiness.

Maybe some will go on to greater heights, naturally. That's great! Maybe some will inspire parents to go on to greater heights - wonderful! But whether it is you or your kid, this needs to come from the true self and the heart and not from wanting and needing. Then we can share joyous achievements.

Resolving and the Interactions: Missing and Subtle

Daily standards

Compulsive behaviours such as working excessive hours, being constantly on a computer or phone, obsessed with sports or even hobbies can seem antisocial or negative to others and may have a detrimental effect on a young kid.

Parents often want to provide the best for their children but sometimes it is better to think about **daily standards** and how to make the most of each day. Daily standards are enjoying the here and now, lessening as much stress as possible and avoiding anxiety about the future.

If you set future goals for a child this can be worrying, especially if they have a gut feeling they won't achieve them. Sometimes the pressure of the goal can prevent them from reaching a good end result.

Kids respond best when those around them are being in the moment because that is how they experience life.

Kids come into the fullness of themselves, achieve to their highest ability and feel happy when all aspects of each day are going well for them. The 6 Steps in this book make this easier to accomplish.

The 10 Second Philosophy by Derek Mills - the standards guy.

Resolving Fear, Invasive Interaction and Control

Fear

Another aspect of Subtle Interaction is a **fear**. Apart from the type of fear parents can get when their kid climbs a tree, there is another fear that can cause distress to your child. It's when a parent needs to use their kid as a buffer in everyday situations like overcoming shyness, reducing their night fears or loneliness.

It works better to be upfront and honest with yourself, those around you and those who can offer help. 'My kid and I are finding life difficult.' You are not alone in feeling this - superficially some may seem to be managing, or putting on a brave face, but deep down most people want change in some or many areas of their life.

Looking after yourself is not selfish or weak. It's practical, like the safety instructions on a plan to 'Put on your own oxygen mask first'.

Kids benefit from sensitive parents so focus on the positive aspects of love with your child. Your child wants to heal any fear in you, both for your sake and so they can feel safer, calmer and more secure, and experience freedom, love and joy.

This can heal the family tree back through many generations and lead to a wonderful journey onward through life for you and your kid.

---

www.felicityevans.co.uk To overcome fear - sources of support for adults.

Invasive Interaction

Invasive Interaction is when a kid experiences your or someone else's anger, fear, disapproval, authority and punishment, unfair restrictions and limitations, or Coercive Control.

Some parents may think that some of the above will help their kid to behave appropriately and be polite, to act in a well brought-up way. These experiences may seem part of learning how to manage life. They may feel that their anger brings a child back to the real world; that fear of what may happen keeps them safe; that disapproval helps them know what is right and what is wrong; that authority and punishment are setting and keeping to boundaries ready for adult life, as are restrictions and limitations.

But neuroscience now proves this not to be so. Usually the opposite happens and kids can fall apart, maybe as a very young child, or in teenage years. They may develop destructive and dysfunctional patterns towards others or themselves, including the full spectrum of obsessive behaviours or addictions. Children or adolescents may use violence and abuse towards a parent. All of these behaviours are a cry for help from a kid suffering huge heartache.

Kids who experience various types of Invasive Interaction from mild to extreme, will be hyper-vigilant. They don't manage life well and may struggle for years. Some may rebel, sometimes with negative consequences. This is different from the natural desire for kids to feel independent and reject the normal family patterns, especially during their teens.

Children need help to recover, to feel less stressed. They consciously need support in creating inner resources, effective communication and positive qualities. This leads to co-operation, excellent self-management and a purposeful lifestyle leading to happiness and success.

Resolving Fear, Invasive Interaction and Control

Coercive Control

Some automatically desire to mould other people, partners or kids, into what they think will make life right for everyone. But control is limiting, and life can become unbearable for those on the receiving end. We can encourage both those who need to control and those on the receiving end to seek compassionate help. **Coercive Control** on others is extreme Invasive Interaction, building up slowly from increasing disapproval and unfair restrictions. This behaviour can stem from neurological differences and how a person has been treated as a child at home or in school.

It can become a powerful pattern of controlling and manipulating people and situations. This can be overt, threatening and angry or passive like not talking, not listening, not helping, withholding money, keeping big secrets. Sometimes control presents as being 'kind': 'You look tired today, I'll take the car keys with me, so you're not tempted to go out. Then you can have a good rest'.

Control is often cutting people off from friends and family. All these types of control need a lot of courage to seek support and professional advice so things can be different.

For people who use control as a coping mechanism, it can seem like normal everyday life. It's a bit like a blind person not knowing what it's like to see. Extreme Coercive Control is present in increasing numbers of families across the full social spectrum, from those living in extreme poverty to those living in prestigious circumstances, from all walks of life, careers and cultures. As it becomes more fully recognised, more understanding and support is available.

Those adults who use Coercive Control need professional support, to manage this type of behaviour that can be so crippling for them and their families. Without awareness, adults or children on the receiving end of Coercive Control can start to feel that they are in the wrong. This can be very damaging. Owl kids crumple when they feel this type of control. Cat kids may become Owl-like. They can't be themselves.

Hence Coercive Control is illegal in the UK, so children and others can be protected.

Tight restrictions and limitations or the withdrawal of loving attention can be very frightening for a child - so different from fair, negotiated agreements which give feelings of safety and security.

Kids who are on the receiving end of Coercive Control may start to use similar controlling behaviours, so it is very important for them to be protected. The 6 Steps in this book give children ways to cope, to be relaxed and happy, bringing about the freedom to be their true delightful selves.

Most of us will know someone on the receiving end of Coercive Control. If we ask, the person on the receiving end will usually say everything is fine. This is easier than focusing on a painful situation which they may have been led to believe is their fault. It isn't. They might even stand up for the person controlling them as they still love them, even if confused by the situation. Just be there for these people when they can turn to you, and check they know who to turn to for their own and their children's safety and wellbeing.

www.dhs.state.or.us/caf/documents/Parenting_in_the_Context_of_Coercive_Control.pdf

www.womensaid.org.uk/womens-aid-launches-coercive-control-toolkit-supported-by-avon/www.thechange-project.org

www.compass4couples.com Making life easier for couples.

www.johnchristianseminars.com Life skills coach, including online, specialising in developing intuitive intelligence and self-esteem.

www.carlrosierjones.com This website is for STRESSED OUT people looking for help.

Resolving Fear, Invasive Interaction and Control

Danger or abuse

If you or your kid ever experience intense ongoing Coercive Control or other emotional **abuse** or might be in physical **danger**, seek immediate professional help. This is your right and your duty for your child. This may seem like it will exacerbate the situation or make it more dangerous but appropriate and effective support will make things better.

Most of those who abuse will have experienced some type of abuse in their own lives, often unrecognised and unsupported. It can stem from neurological differences which interfere with communication, managing life and the ability to love unconditionally. This makes everyday life impossible for some.

Stress to the level of abuse happens to more people than we realize, at home or work. If people share their difficulties, without seeing one as being in the wrong and the other a victim to this, we can create solutions. We can't change other adults - that is up to them. We can explore useful information about challenging situations and develop an understanding of the causes, changing our attitudes towards the joint situation.

A child will eventually show their distress at a situation that isn't working for them. They may be desperate for change and they need ongoing support from someone in the family or school. If they are not supported this commonly leads to self-destructive patterns in themselves.

Challenges can pass on between generations, each time getting more marked. Let's resolve problems now. We all have the kindness gene and 'happiness is a skill that can be learnt'.

---

www.womensaid.org.uk

www.thechange-project.org

Understanding Pathological Demand Avoidance Syndrome by Phil Christie, Margaret Duncan, Ruth Fiddler, Zara Healy. PDA causes a neurological compulsion to control, and rage when control breaks down.

A Painful Gift by Christopher Goodchild, a late diagnosis of Asperger's.

Resolving Lack of Interaction and Sensitivity

Lack of Interaction

Lack of Interaction is also when you can't intervene to change things for your kid so you sort of have to go into denial to make a quieter life for you and, you believe, them.

This denial usually needs professional help. Seeking support is spreading the word about difficulties to families and friends, increasing understanding of varied problems and thereby increasing solutions. Asking for help is making more help available to others. Find the courage to say to someone who will listen 'Right now my kid and I need help.'

If you can't do this face to face, find an online forum to gain further information and support so you can start to open up. This is a new and valuable resource and the more who use it, the more effective it can be.

---

www.womensaid.org.uk For support and change that lasts.

www.fixers.org.uk Young people working with their past to innovate their futures.

Resolving Lack of Interaction and Sensitivity

You too were sensitive to a degree

If you have a kid who is particularly sensitive, it is very likely that **you too were sensitive to a degree** in some or many ways, even if you managed life, work and friendship well on the surface.

It might be that you didn't get the full understanding, nurturing, loving, communicating, resolving and playing to bring you to the fullness of yourself.

So having a kid may be your chance to revisit understanding, nurturing, loving, communicating, resolving and playing for yourself as well as your kid.

Resolving Lack of Interaction and Sensitivity

Parents to be fully present

Sometimes sensitivities in adults have become too disorientating, confusing or painful and it becomes difficult to manage everyday life with ease, causing some to resort to self-medicating with alcohol or drugs, or a wide range of self-destructive behaviours. This isn't always extreme use - it can be smoking, overeating, or actions like working excessive hours. Self-medication is trying to find a way to cope. Other choices may not have been available.

Self-medication may seem to make life easier for some adults but children often have a profound feeling that a parent self-medicating is not fully present for them. They learn about cigarettes, alcohol and drugs endangering health and become worried.

Then they feel that the world isn't a safe place to live in. So as a society we need to give understanding, compassion and support, ideally before children use negative behaviours as cries for help themselves. It is especially

important to stop blaming those kids who are seen as 'naughty' or challenging. There will be a reason.

We can also help kids understand that it is OK to love a person, even when they feel very worried or don't like what that person is doing.

Kids want their **parents to be fully present** with them rather than to be under the influence of substances or waiting for the next cigarette. Children notice mood changes.

Whatever your lifestyle, take time to be fully present with your kid so you can enjoy happy, quality time. Your kid loves, wants and needs the real you.

The Inner Fix by Persia Lawson and Joanne Bradford.

www.addictivedaughter.com

www.alcoholicsanonymous.org.uk For those who want to change drinking patterns.

www.al-anonuk.org.uk For those who are affected by someone else's drinking patterns.

www.michaeljames.be

www.actionforhappiness.org

www.johnchristianseminars.com

www.carlrosierjones.com

Resolving Lack of Interaction and Sensitivity

'Handing Over'

Sometimes it can seem that resolving problems with kids or other aspects of life is impossible. Life feels like it's going from bad to worse!

To have a problem in the first place can be seen by some as weakness, ineptitude, laziness or stupidity. But it's not. It is a message. Problems, pains and heartache are messages to make us aware, to swing the pendulum towards better outcomes.

It's good to find ways to stop old patterns of excessive worry, anxiety and fear getting in the way. These can send us back into a pit of despair, or back into denial.

So how can we gradually see light at the end of the tunnel? Some people wake up feeling anxious – usually a physical lack of wellbeing. We can build good physical health. This is very fashionable with loads of choices. Vitality is the opposite of depression. Remember, the brain has

neuroplasticity so we can unlock it to being in the moment and having creative ideas! There are ways to explore this, like mindfulness.

After exceptional trauma, some gain peace by surrendering. In everyday life this can be practised by **'Handing Over'**. Sometimes we can't control situations. We can only change ourselves.

Neuroscience shows that 'Handing Over' has a powerful effect on the brain and the body. Writing down what we want to 'Hand Over' in a structured way just works! We can practise this with the daily aspects of life so it becomes easier when we want to apply it to harder challenges.

'Handing Over' sets the pendulum in motion for solutions and moving from heartache to happiness with a strong sense of self. We can share this with our kids.

---

www.michaeljames.be 'Handing over' groups in London and Brighton.

www.museumofhappiness.org 'Happiness is a learnt skill', Shamash Alidina.

www.felicityevans.co.uk See Instruction sheet for 'Handing Over'.

Resolving Lack of Interaction and Sensitivity

Kids carry on loving

Resolving can feel like hard work for some adults. In reality you may feel exhausted, frustrated or stressed so it seems impossible to find the energy for things to be different.

First find ways to recharge, to relax and have more fun and laughter. Feel better on the inside. Playing is the next Step in this book and your play is equally as important as your kid's.

The Resolving pages came from what parents say about their own lives and what kids are expressing in words or actions. Adults can hang onto their stresses for years.

Children need Resolving to happen quickly in their lives or some refuse to co-operate, others may express profound anger or withdraw to crisis level. Some children can't learn and a few may be excluded from school.

A tiny step towards Resolving can open up the path for change within you and with the children.

Whatever their outer world is like, even when they are raging or withdrawing or running away, deep inside **our kids carry on loving**. They want to laugh, have fun and play with you.

On the next page is a story by Emma, a child who couldn't write stories in school. One day she painted a beautiful picture. I asked her if she would like to write something about it …

Emma's story

The Pathway

My picture reminds me of a long journey up the beautiful, flowery pathway. In some ways it makes me think of my family, and what we are going through, but in other ways it reminds me of a little caterpillar. It starts off at the bottom with all the beautiful flowers and everything is happy. Then gradually you begin your journey up the stony, brown pathway. Things start to get harder and harder for you as the hill gets steeper. The flowers get smaller, the days get darker. The weather's changing. The flowers are changing and you are changing. When you look up the hill it seems like it will never end.

Then it gets too much. You start to get these outbursts of rage and anger. When you feel like this, it's like everything you do is the end of the world. So you lock away. You lock away into a dark, sheltered cocoon, where no-one can see you, where you are all alone, to think about what you have gone through, and to restart, and just think about going for your dream.

Then after weeks or days or maybe even years, the cocoon breaks! You come out as a beautiful butterfly at the top of the pathway. You have beautiful, coloured wings to fly away and touch your dream. When you are at the top of the pathway you can see all the beautiful flowers around you and you'll know that all your troubles are behind you.

Emma wrote this story from her heart, finding her courage to break through her heartache. Many children, even little ones, show or talk to me about this type of heartache. All want to create a beautiful feeling inside themselves - one of wellbeing, resilience, love, laughter, fun and joy.

www.felicityevans.co.uk See Heartache to Happiness Box.

Playing

'Let's blow bubbles.'

Playing

Introduction

Play is the foundation of communication and learning.

This is the section that can flow easily for parents and kids, especially once the other 5 Steps are working well. Play is also the area that can support understanding, nurturing, loving, communicating and resolving.

Most of this section is written for young children but each idea can be adapted for teenagers. We all benefit from our **power activity, time to be, personal space, experiencing the elements**, and **5 quick ways to feel OK**.

These ideas may already be usual occurrences for you. But some kids need specific focus, planning, organisation and time to play purposefully and harmoniously.

NatureKids started with a small group of kids who couldn't play together. Gradually they created activities that they enjoyed and in their words 'became a family'. New kids arrived who were distressed in some way but gradually joined in, even streetwise teenagers! I saw their wellbeing grow and happiness increase.

With play for little ones, and teenagers in a different way, it helps to think about whether your kid is predominantly 'Cat' or 'Owl', as explained at the start of this book. If you have siblings that are opposite Owl and Cat types, seek to help them find a common ground. They need the place, structure or situation to first play in their own ways, alongside one another. Generalising, Owls like to ponder and dawdle first. Cats like to chat and rush into things. Cat kids often need to chat to someone. Then once both kids are relaxed, they will enjoy joining in with each other's play.

Here are activities and strategies that provide cheap, easy fun.

Effective play and leisure can last a lifetime. It's never too late to have a happy childhood! Play can be fun for adults too!

Playing Contents

Playing Ideas

Playing as a Power Activity

Playing with the Elements

Playing to build a deeper sense of self

Playing Ideas

Take time to 'blow bubbles'

Take time to 'blow bubbles' with your kid.

Sometimes it might be a time to completely relax and chill out.

Other times it might be explorative, like finding ways to make square bubbles. Have you ever tried pointing a hairdryer at bubbles? Used kitchen utensils to make bubbles? Or made giant bubbles like the ones you see adults blowing in the park?

'Time to blow bubbles' includes any activity that is light-hearted and fun for you both and not essential to daily life. But it is definitely experiential.

Watch out for as many of these special activities as possible and have the next ones ready as your child grows up - see the link below!

All kids may have periods when they seem not to need or want these times but if you are ready, they will usually return to them.

Owls like you to be feeling good whilst 'blowing bubbles'.

Cats like the 'bubbles' to be fun.

Both want to have a loving experience.

www.uk.pinterest.com/explore/bubble-crafts/ Bubble fun for all ages, including teens and adults!

Playing Ideas

Shared pleasures

Consider the activity that you most enjoy doing with your kid - the one that they thoroughly enjoy doing too. Ensure that you have **shared pleasures.**

What activities do you both like doing? Going for a walk, maybe with a pedometer, or Geocaching? Cooking familiar or unusual recipes? Maybe making raw food nibbles, like blended dates and cashews? Drawing or colouring? There are plenty of adult colouring sheets online. Jigsaws - like 3D metal ones, to build together? Have you tried Geomag which is very popular with kids and adults? Making a model? Some kids will play for hours with junk boxes and often appreciate help with the glue. Stimulating imaginary games with dressing up clothes or interesting objects? Is your kid's 'screen time' proactive and sometimes interactive and fun for you?

Sometimes the activity can be alone with your child, simple things like cuddling up or relaxing with a film. At other times it can be spending fun time with other children or adults, like having a picnic or going bowling.

These activities will change over the years. Check that you always have one in your mind, especially for the days that your kid really needs a special time with you. Maybe have a place in town or nearby where you can be on your own to relax and chat together.

Owls are reactive to what is going on and will escalate your feelings, whatever they are.

Cats are proactive and will enhance the activity.

Playing Ideas

Joke moments

Most kids love jokes, even before they get the punch line. Have a few joke books around the house and share some **joke moments** with your kid.

Jokes are especially useful during times when a distraction is needed like getting dressed or washing up. They are also useful for diffusing tension and uplifting atmospheres.

Joke moments can go on for many years!

Cats love words and jokes!

Owls like the feeling of fun and the smile on your face, even if the joke means nothing to them!

Playing Ideas

Make a nice surprise

Help your kid to **make a nice surprise** for someone as often as possible: a painted or drawn place mat; collected flowers, leaves or twigs; an interesting stone; special food; a junk model; a song to sing.

This isn't to make your kid into a goody-goody!

It is to give them the experience of positive reactions from people.

Life can be full of demands and kids can find it tricky to get life right at times. So, if they practise the experiences that get good reactions, this puts life in balance and helps them to manage the trickier aspects of life.

It is focusing on fun and enjoyment and seeing a look of pleasure and appreciation on someone else's face.

This is natural joint activity for Cats.
They like what they have made to look good.

Owls do best when it is self-initiated or when they are given subtle support. It has to feel right for them.

Playing Ideas

Treasure table, shelf or box

Set up a **treasure table, shelf or box**. Models, drawings or collected items can go on display here to give your kid the pleasure of showing you and others.

This makes for easy, happy communication for little ones. Then that experience goes on to give confidence to older kids and leads towards effective communication throughout life.

It's when play can build a sense of community and self-worth.

Check this is not embarrassing for an Owl, or if they have passed the moment of interest. They may need a new collection daily.

Cats may want to overfill the table and hoard everything.

Playing Ideas

Camp or personal space

Make a **camp or personal space** with your kid, indoors or outside. Sometimes they may want to hide away here quietly. At other times they may ask you to come in and share time with them or want to play with friends.

It can be a quick camp, like a rug over a table, or pinned to the garden fence.

Older children can have a great time spending ages making intricate camps.

Some kids like to hide away when they are angry, stressed, emotionally overwhelmed or in sensory overload. Hiding away is a positive way for them to settle themselves and feel better.

Always reinforce this type of self-regulating back to OK with kind, positive words.

We all need our personal spaces.

Owls and Cats, of all ages, love camps and personal spaces.

Playing Ideas

Fun meal

Have a healthy **fun meal**.

The food could be arranged into a face, or flower, or boat shape.

Choose the healthiest foods that your kid likes.

Some like to write out or draw menus.

You could have a finger picnic in their camp, on a rug in the living room or any unusual place. When there's time, going off to the park, woods or seaside is especially great.

Your kid's body and brain are made up of what they eat and drink so one aim may be to increase the amount of healthy food they eat.

Fun meals can encourage healthy eating.

Super Food Family Classics by Jamie Oliver.

Raw Magic by Kate Magic.

Hemsley and Hemsley: The Art of Eating Well by Jasmine and Melissa Hemsley.

Playing as a Power Activity

Imagination and creativity

Many kids do better with an old box rather than specific toys because this fuels their imagination. **Imagination and creativity** are crucial for a kid's wellbeing and happiness.

Some blossom with art and crafts or have natural musical talents but many just enjoy 'making and doing' in their own unique way.

If you provide the opportunity and stuff for your kid to explore, they will show you what brings them satisfaction.

Encourage this fuelling of the imagination, exploration, passion and interest over the years as not only does it mean less boredom but it is also developing a creativity that can overcome stresses and problems and lead to an open mindset. That in turn makes life much easier and more enjoyable.

Cats will mainly want their activity to have a lot of verbal content and interaction.

Owls may prefer solitary play in their own world.

Probably check that your kid has opportunity for both, so they can come into a good balance and harmony.

Playing as a Power Activity

Power activity

Watch out for and encourage your kid's **power activity**.

This is when they become animated - their eyes light up as they come into the fullness and positive power of themselves.

Power activities can last a moment, a few days or longterm and they can be anything: climbing a tree, jumping into a pool, a sport, painting a cardboard box, loom bands, cooking (aim for healthy cooking as unhealthy food can end up as depowering), performing, stroking a pet, accomplishing an amazing feat.

Power activities build inner strengths, security and wellbeing that can continue for a lifetime.

Playing as a Power Activity

Supervision and guidance

If your kid's power activity is trying to get the tortoise out of its shell or unscrewing the taps on a boat, this isn't going to work for them, the tortoise, or the boat !

Increase your **supervision and guidance** by giving them more attention and explaining why something may not be appropriate, before they do something wrong.

Divert and encourage their exploration - maybe by giving them an old clock to take apart instead of the tortoise and loads of exciting water play like damming a stream.

It's so much easier if you pre-empt and give kids lots of exciting adventures rather than them always ending up doing something destructive for the tortoise, themselves or someone else.

The earlier kids are encouraged onto a path through life that gives them positive acknowledgment and that works for everyone, the stronger this path becomes.

Playing as a Power Activity

Use screens in a beneficial and fun way

If your kid discovers their Power Activities and has regular and easy access to them, this fills some of their time and encourages them to **use computers, phones and screens in a beneficial and fun way.**

If other important needs such as being fully present with your child, outdoor time and friendship are met, computers won't become a problem, an obsession or addiction. Meeting a child's needs first can avoid years of ongoing problems, tantrums and stress from trying to get them off a computer.

When used as escapism, computers are not beneficial.

When used proactively, they remain a source of information, healthy connections and pleasure.

Playing as a Power Activity

Love music in their own way

Ideally kids let us know when they want to explore music and we can facilitate this. If they don't show interest, suggestions can be made.

But it's really important for kids to **love music in their own way** rather than you wanting your child to become musical. Check that any musical experiences you offer them remain pleasurable. Avoid nagging about music practice or the cost of a music exam. Music is an inner joy, sometimes just for oneself, sometimes shared.

Playing a musical instrument or singing may be a huge, natural talent. It may even become a career. Just let this develop naturally.

Music can help a child to connect with their heart and their feelings and encourage expression.

Sometimes certain songs may be special, either because of the words or music.

Watching a child's interest in music often gives an insight into their thoughts and feelings. Some can play with music for hours.

From quite young, kids can pick up the 'feel' of music, and a very mature understanding of the gist of a song, even if they don't follow all the words.

Music can be relaxing to induce sleep.

It might even encourage learning and intelligence.

Music and songs can give security and calm, uplift and entertain, and bring happiness into all our lives.

Playing with the Elements

Love the elements

Most kids **love the elements**: earth, air, fire, water.

If your kid is over feisty and fiery, settle them with a water or earthy activity.

If they are over-emotional or weepy, fire can balance them.

If they are dreamy and airy, ground them with earth activities and help them express their feelings with gentle water time.

If they are stubborn, dogmatic and earthy, help them feel lighter by being in contact with air.

Playing with the Elements

Fire to be safe

Fire is often the element that children need most.

Rather than steer your kid away from fire, it is good to give them sufficient supervision for **fire to be safe** and this can start from quite a young age.

Ideally this is something like a small bonfire in the garden, which they can poke a stick in and set it alight, learning that the end they are holding is cold and safe but the other end is hot and can burn.

This teaches about the dangers of sparklers and that they should be put in a bucket of sand as soon as they finish.

Small fireworks can give huge enjoyment when kids are old enough to learn how to light their own small ones safely. Indoors the fireworks for birthday cakes can be fun, again with high supervision, opening windows so the fumes are not inhaled by young lungs.

Lighting and blowing out a candle can encourage learning about how to use a match safely.

Kids who can experience fire safely tend to do less dangerous fire play behind adults' backs.

Playing with the Elements

Earth can provide safe and satisfying play

Earth can provide safe and satisfying play for a small child, once they stop eating it!

This can be as simple as poking a stick in earth or mixing water and earth to make mud pies.

Most kids love walking, jumping and skidding in mud and getting dirty.

Those who don't may need help to be less scared of mud, as this can lead on to other fears like getting paint on their hands or even more marked phobias.

Washing muddy clothes and having to put your kid in the bath may seem a hassle but if getting muddy relaxes your kid and makes them happy, it becomes very worthwhile.

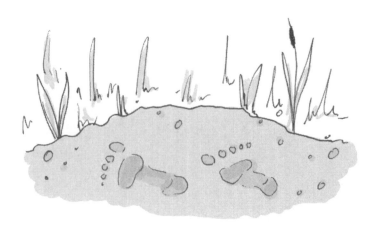

Playing with the Elements

Air activities

Air activities are less tangible but most kids like air.

They love to feel wind blowing through their hair, being on top of a hill in the breeze and to be out in a gale when they are almost being blown over.

Remind kids not to play in the woods or climb a tree when there is a gale.

Kids love hanging onto a kite, seeing bubbles race off into the sky, catching falling leaves.

Air can give a sense of lightness and freedom.

Playing with the Elements

Water play

Providing lots of **water play** and experiences can build water awareness and safety.

Kids who live near deep water may tend to naturally develop a cautious attitude and this is better than a fear, which can lead to unpredictable or dangerous behaviours near water.

Love of water and learning how to swim is important for all children. But check swimming is always an absolute pleasure. Some lessons can put kids off swimming for life. All kids need to learn to swim in a way that suits them.

Most kids enjoy pond dipping.

Bathtime with loads of things to occupy your kid (or music, candles and some essential oils as they get older) is a perfect way to relax a stroppy, tired, overloaded or overwhelmed kid and it needn't necessarily be kept for the end of the day.

Bathtime is great for recharging kids when they are exhausted from a long school day. After a bath they can put on their pyjamas, then a track suit or similar over the top, ready for play. This leaves less to do at bedtime. It can work very well at times, especially for little ones.

Water pistols can be huge fun and you can set up targets, if you don't want to be drenched. This is a time to practice boundaries too, like an agreement that water must be squirted in safe places, not eyes. Also there can be an agreement on appropriate ways and times - maybe just on legs and not soaking you just as you are about to go shopping.

Playing to build a deeper sense of self

Especially friendly

If possible, make a point of being **especially friendly** to people: other kids, shopkeepers, teachers, friends and relatives.

Some adults may be naturally shy, although I see this as being open-hearted and sensitive to others.

But if you can act being sociable and friendly, even just a little, this is a good way to encourage happy play and good relationships for your child.

It shows them that you like people and this increases children's security and gives them better feelings about themselves.

Life gets easier when we can manage being friendly to a wide range of people.

Playing to build a deeper sense of self

Absorbed on their own

Ensure that your kid can play happily and be **absorbed on their own** so they don't need attention from someone else all the time.

Owls will most likely do this naturally: arranging play people, drawing or making something.

Cats may need help to take time to play by themselves. Be aware that if they're asked to play on their own, they may find this too stressful unless they feel like it and are ready to be creative.

Initially Cats usually want your company. So it's worth setting aside some time for them to settle to an activity. Then you can say you are just going to do some jobs but will come back in a little while - this may need to be very short to start with and increased gradually. For some it works if you record yourself reading a story for them to listen to while you get on with something else. Or you can use music, a TV programme, DVD or story for them to listen to until they become absorbed in an activity.

Playing on their own builds inner strength and resilience in kids, which helps them mature and enjoy time to themselves throughout life.

Playing to build a deeper sense of self

Time to be

Encourage your kid to have **time to be.**

This is different from playing on their own.

This is creating a natural opportunity for kids to chill out without any demands, without having to concentrate on doing or achieving anything. If the evening is hectic with homework and chores to be done, set the timer for 10 minutes when no demands are made. This gives you a break too.

'Time to be' can be encouraged and expanded by giving kids time and space, including physical and emotional space.

Being out of doors, especially in Nature, encourages 'time to be': poking a stick in mud, hanging on a swing, sitting in a tree, drawing with a stick in sand.

Indoors it can be relaxing under a table covered by a blanket, watching a fire, sitting in a bubble bath with lavender oil, maybe a candle.

It's a sort of day-dreaming time, time to be comfortable in their thoughts or imagination - mindfulness for kids.

Does this sound tempting? 'Time to be' is crucial for adults too!

Enjoying 'time to be' is important for development and health and wellbeing in later life.

Playing to build a deeper sense of self

Be together

Your kid also needs time to be with other kids, where there is no adult-led or structured activity. They can just **be together**, ideally outdoors whatever the weather, for some of the time.

Out of school activities like Cubs, Brownies, football, swimming lessons or similar activities have benefits, but the structure can seem similar to school.

Nowadays, as playing out is not the norm, some kids need this to be timetabled into their week.

They need as much free time like this as possible - just to play and be with other kids.

Being with other kids, having the freedom to explore, create and communicate is both an important part of learning and a crucial aspect of emotional maturation and wellbeing.

Playing to build a deeper sense of self

Quality playing time

Ensure your kid experiences and enjoys lots of **quality playing time**, time for discovering the world around them, and building a deeper sense of true inner self.

This isn't an indulgence. For all ages play is crucial for relaxation and recharge, energy and vitality, and fun.

With kids, play can enhance development, learning, communication and friendship.

Your kid will thrive with play as times of problem-solving, dealing with feelings, passion and enthusiasm, creativity and invention, peace and quiet, loving and joyous experiences with others.

Playing is a way to practise these qualities - ones which not only lead to internal resilience but strength of character and fulfilling potential in the actual world.

Many adults have written about their talents developing as they 'played outside with their friends'.

When your child has quality play, you can observe them being in happiness and each happy day builds an inner reserve for the future.

Playing to build a deeper sense of self

5 quick checks to help your kid feel playful and OK

How are you and everyone else in the house feeling?

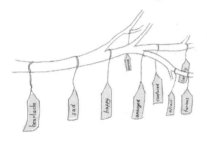

Are you able to be fully present?

Have you done some fun activities?

Has your kid had loads of time to be, preferably outside?

Have you role-modelled unconditional love and reminded your child that you love them?

Playing to build a deeper sense of self

Enjoy today!

With these 6 steps of
Understanding, Nurturing,
Loving, Communicating,
Resolving and Playing, you
are making our world and
life in general much easier
for your kid, and you! Follow
these Steps and kids will truly
thrive in our world today.

This reduces your stress,
worry and fatigue.

As you build your child's
wellbeing and inner resilience,
this strengthens yours.

When kids are fully being
themselves rather than living
with expectations put on
them by others, their innate
talents surface and as they
develop these, they really
enjoy their achievements.
This leads to success, often in
unexpected ways.

May your kid discover more
of themselves through play,
be able to let go of heartache,
experience happiness, share
lots of unconditional love
with you and others, and
enjoy today!

Feeling good is our natural
way of being!

If you are reading this page before the rest of the book, I encourage you to start at the beginning!

If you need to repeat and really 'do' any page, I wish you the courage to do this.

For extra support, you can turn to my website: www.felicityevans.co.uk.

If you have carried out all 6 Steps, you will start to feel more relaxed and have frequent big smiles!

Spread the word about what is possible.

Thank you,

Felicity.

Thank you for looking at this book.

You now have about 170 ideas: some new, some where you shout 'YES', some puzzling and a few that trigger heartache - the message to swing the pendulum to happiness. The innovative suggestions are quickly becoming mainstream because we can't keep repeating old patterns that aren't working with our kids. These ideas can easily change family dynamics and heal the family tree.

First have patience with your kid and, more importantly, yourself. I took 50 years to be aware of all these ideas! My son started building my awareness from a very young age and hundreds of kids have carried on since then.

I introduce you to my sources of support, so you are not alone. You now have the information to make life easier and happier for your child as they grow up. Maybe just a few of these suggestions will help your child to be healthier, to find school easier or cope with rejection from a 'friend'. We can aim for the fun times with our kids that build wellbeing.

Have courage for yourself and your kid - the courage that builds inner resilience in them. Encourage them to develop as themselves, however they may be presenting to the world now. Ask your child's school to enable them feel self-worth, by setting realistic goals. School should be fun, interesting and a pleasurable part of growing up.

Experience hope and know that it is real so you can exude this to your children and validate it for them with their experiences.

All the strategies and ideas in this book work towards building patience, courage and hope, for you and your kid to create a strong sense of self, immense wellbeing, joy and happiness. Then children blossom and thrive.

End of book resources

Links to other useful sites and therapies

www.felicityevans.co.uk My website with support, information and articles for parents, teachers, adults, teens and kids. For some parents the questionnaires on this site may help you more fully understand your kid and get support.

Wellbeing and Health
www.indigoessences.com E.g. for confidence, to help sleep, to overcome fear.
www.naet.com For allergies, intolerances, to eliminate toxins and enable better absorption of nutrients.
www.cease-therapy.com A homeopathic programme to help autistic kids, but also good for other symptoms and stresses.
bob@accesspotential.net Neuro-developmental therapy. Also see the questionnaire at **www.felicityevans.co.uk**
www.imperfectlynatural.com Leading a natural life for yourself and kids.
www.azulfit.com For recipe e book: Truly Healthy, Truly Delicious, Jo Dombernowsky
www.drdavidhamilton.com Using science to inspire.
www.addictivedaughter.com Be stronger, happier, braver.
www.babo.co.uk Behavioural optometrists.
www.functionalmedicine.org GPs who look at the root causes of all problems.
www.vantullekenbrothers.com The doctor who gave up drugs.
www.homeopathyeurope.org
www.bcma.co.uk The British Complementary Medicine Association.

Education
Ken Robinson: Ted Talk, changing education paradigms:
www.ted.com/talks/ken_robinson_changing_education_paradigms
www.charactereducation.co A headteacher's advice on developing good character.
http://jubileecentre.ac.uk/1635/character-education. Character curriculum in schools.
Educating Ruby, by Bill Lucas and Guy Claxton.
ISBN-10: 1845909542, ISBN-13: 978-1845909543.

Support
www.unschoolingaspies.blogspot.co.uk An Avenue Mum blogging the differences.
www.naturaldads.com Great for Mums too!
www.compass4couples.com MOT for couples to get back to fun and joy.
www.rodwellhypnotherapy.co.uk Fulfil your potential, release obstacles and pain.

www.autismangels.co.uk Pony experiences.

www.aspergerexperts.com Run by those who share their own experiences of Asperger's, including the causes of meltdowns.

www.virtuesproject.com Helpful for finding the right words to use or share with your kid or on a family poster, e.g. generous, kind, careful.

www.childbereavementuk.org

www.mermaidsuk.org.uk Family support for children with gender identity issues.

www.autism.org.uk

www.dyslexiaaction.org.uk

www.womensaid.org.uk National Domestic Violence Helpline 0808 2000 247.

www.thechange-project.org

www.dhs.state.or.us/caf/documents/Parenting_in_the_Context_of_Coercive_Control.pdf

www.womensaid.org.uk/womens-aid-launches-coercive-control-toolkit-supported-by-avon/

www.alcoholics-anonymous.org.uk

www.al-anonuk.org.uk For those who are affected by someone else's alcohol patterns.

Booklist

Sitting Still like a Frog by Eline Snel, book with a CD. ISBN-13: 978-1611800586.

The Gardener and the Carpenter by Alison Gopnik. What the new science of child development tells us about the relationship between parents and children. ISBN-13: 978-1847921611.

The Whole-Brain Child by Dr Daniel Siegel and Dr Tina Payne Bryson. ISBN-13: 978-1780338378.

No-Drama Discipline by Dr Daniel Siegel and Dr Tina Payne Bryson. ISBN-13: 978-1922247568.

Magic Eyes by Leo Angart. ISBN-13: 978-1845909598.

The Highly Sensitive Child by Elaine Aron. ISBN-13: 978-0007163939.

The Children of Now by Dr Meg Blackburn Losey. ISBN-13: 978-1564149480.

Ungifted by Scott Barry Kaufman. ASIN: B00ZT1LACM.

The Indigo Survival Guide by Olena MA Gill. ASIN: B00DIKX380.

Indigo Children by Lee Carroll and Jan Tober. ISBN-13: 978-1561706082.

Imperfectly Natural Baby and Toddler by Janey Lee Grace. ISBN-13: 978-0752885896.

Understanding Pathological Demand Avoidance Syndrome by Phil Christie, Margaret Duncan, Ruth Fiddler, Zara Healy. ISBN-13: 978-1849050746.

Books showing the acute awareness of kids who experience life in very different ways:
Sensory overload robs me of my moral code by Harry Thompson. An open and honest account of childhood to adulthood with PDA.
The Reason I Jump by Naoki Higashida ISBN-13: 978-1444776775.
The Spark by Kristine Barnet ISBN-13: 978-0241145623.
The Horse Boy by Rupert Isaacson ISBN-13: 978-0141033631.
The Long Ride Home by Rupert Isaacson. ISBN-13: 978-0670922284.
A Boy Made of Blocks by Keith Stuart. A novel inspired by Keith's experiences with his son. ISBN 978-0751563290.

Books showing the acute awareness of adults who experience life in very different ways:
Thinking in Pictures (and other books) by Temple Grandin. ISBN-13: 978-0747585329.
A Painful Gift by Christopher Goodchild: late diagnosis of Asperger's. ISBN-13: 978-0232527582.

How childhood affects adulthood:
Childhood Disrupted: How Your Biography Becomes Your Biology, and How You Can Heal by Donna Jackson Nakazawa. ISBN-13: 978-1476748368.

Books for Adults:
The Caveman Principles: Get rid of everyday stress and enjoy mammoth success! by Carl Rosier-Jones. ISBN-13: 978-1910819395. Great for family communication and dynamics.
I Heart Me by David Hamilton. ISBN-13: 978-1781801840. Establishing self-love, plus other books and CDs.
The Inner Fix: be stronger, happier and braver by Persia Lawson and Joanne Bradford. ISBN-13: 978-1473620209.
The Coupledom Trap by Tal Araim. ISBN 978-1-911425-53-3. Have the courage to be honest and guide yourself away from the stereotypical trap and into happiness.
The Element: How finding your passion changes everything by Ken Robinson. ISBN-13: 978-0141045252.
The Loneliness Cure: 6 strategies for finding real connections in your life by Kory Floyd, MD. ISBN-13: 978-1440582097.
Presence by Patsy Rodenburg. ISBN-13: 978-0141039473. Presence is a great gift to give your child.

Dying to be me by Anita Moorjani. ISBN-13: 978-1848507838. The importance of being ourselves, and letting young people be themselves, and to not be afraid of death.
Out of the Darkness by Steve Taylor. ISBN-13: 978-1848502543. Awakening after intense trauma and inner turmoil.
Healing without Freud or Prozac by Dr David Servan Shreiber. ISBN-13: 978-1447211464.
Mindset by Carol Dweck. ISBN-13: 978-1780332000. Exploring fixed and growth mindsets
Love is Letting Go of Fear by Gerald G Jampolsky. ISBN-13: 978-1587611186.
The 10 Second Philosophy by Derek Mills. ISBN-13: 978-1848509788. A practical guide to success and happiness.
Nutrition:
Everyday Superfood by Jamie Oliver. ISBN-13: 978-0718181239.
Raw Magic by Kate Magic ISBN-13: 978-1934170373.
Hemsley and Hemsley: The Art of Eating Well by Jasmine and Melissa Hemsley. ISBN-13: 978-0091958329.

Groups, coaching, action

www.michaeljames.be Emerging journeys.
It doesn't matter how you are feeling, you can always feel better. Michael offers practical and groundbreaking ideas for enjoying life, from feeling low, feeling uninspired or feeling good to creating the life you want.
www.actionforhappiness.org Helps people take action for a happier and more caring world, and runs local support groups.
www.johnchristianseminars.com Life skills coach, including online, specialising in developing intuitive intelligence and self-esteem.
www.carlrosierjones.com This website is for STRESSED OUT people looking for help.
www.janeyleegrace.com/one-to-one-coaching-with-janey-lee-grace/ For clarity and vision.
www.brahmakumaris.org Courses for managing anger.
www.derekmills.com Succeed in life without setting goals. Set standards instead.
www.fixers.org.uk Young people working with their past to innovate their futures.

Printed in Great Britain
by Amazon